VANCOUVER ISLAND TRAVEL GUIDE 2025

Your Ultimate Companion for an Unforgettable Adventure

Kelly D. Farrell

Copyright

Copyright 2024 Kelly D. Farrell. All rights reserved. No part of this publication may be reproduced, distributed, or transmitted in any form or by any means, including photocopying, recording, or other electronic or mechanical methods, without the prior written permission of the copyright owner.

Table of Contents

Introduction
    A Memorable Journey Through Vancouver Island's Wonders
    Brief History and Cultural Heritage
    When to Visit: Seasons and Events
    Planning Your Trip
Chapter 2
    Exploring Vancouver Island's Regions
Chapter 3
    Natural Wonders and Outdoor Adventures
Chapter 4
    Cultural Experiences and First Nations Heritage
Chapter 5
    Culinary Delights of Vancouver Island
Chapter 6
    Urban Exploration and Shopping
Chapter 7
    Family-Friendly Activities and Attractions
Chapter 8
    Practical Information for Visitors
Chapter 9
    Off the Beaten Path: Hidden Gems and Unique Experiences
Conclusion

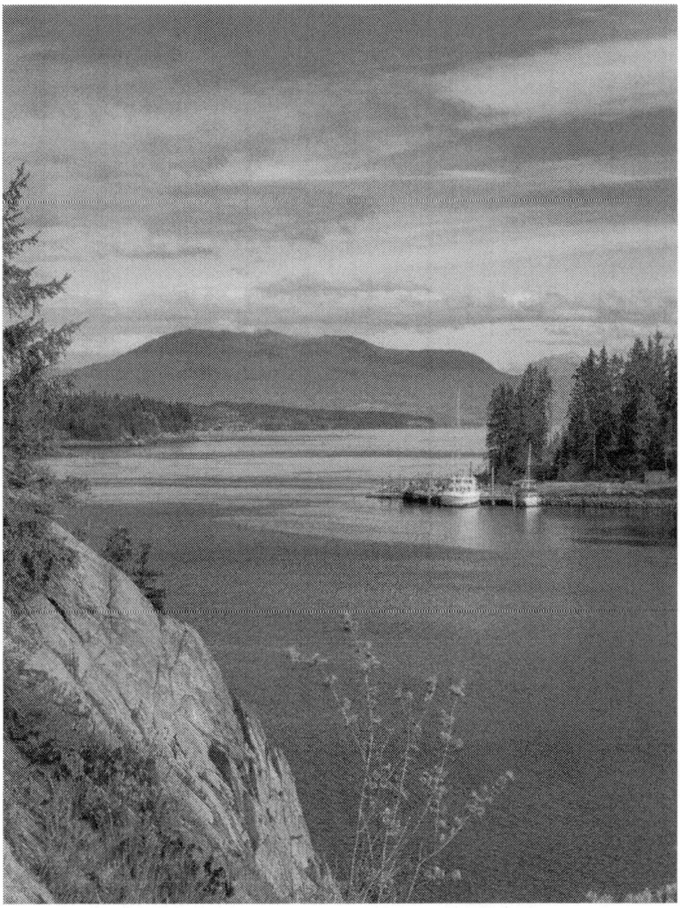

Introduction

A Memorable Journey Through Vancouver Island's Wonders

As I stepped off the ship onto Vancouver Island soil, a rush of anticipation and exhilaration washed over me. The cold Pacific air entered my lungs, bringing with it the aroma of pine and saltwater. Little did I realize that this island beauty would capture my heart and leave me with lifelong memories.

My journey began in Victoria, the picturesque capital city of British Columbia. The Inner Harbour welcomed me with breathtaking views of seaplanes taking off and landing against a backdrop of historic structures. The renowned Fairmont Empress Hotel stood proudly, enticing me to partake in their famed afternoon tea. As I sipped Earl Grey and ate dainty sandwiches, I looked out at the lively waterfront, where street entertainers entertained visitors.

I went to the Royal British Columbia Museum, eager to learn about the island's rich cultural legacy. The First Peoples Gallery provides a remarkable glimpse into the ancient cultures that have inhabited this region for thousands of years. Detailed totem poles, ceremonial masks, and interactive exhibits brought the stories of the Coast Salish, Nuu-chah-nulth, and Kwakwaka'wakw peoples to life.

Driving out of the city, I took the picturesque Malahat Drive, which winds through lush forests and offers views of the Saanich Inlet far below. My destination was Cowichan Valley, also known as Vancouver Island's wine area. I had a wonderful afternoon visiting vineyards, sipping crisp whites and strong reds, and talking with enthusiastic winemakers about their profession.

As the sun sank, I found myself in Chemainus, a charming town known for its outdoor mural gallery. Walking through the streets seemed like entering a living art display, with bright paintings representing the area's history and culture covering every building wall.

The next day, I traveled west towards Tofino, passing through the center of Vancouver Island. The journey itself was an experience, with towering trees bordering the twisting route and occasional glimpses of lovely lakes peering through the greenery. As I approached the Pacific Rim, the terrain changed radically. Ancient jungles gave way to craggy coasts, and the air became dense with ocean mist.

Tofino, a little surf town on the border of the forest, greeted me with a relaxed atmosphere and breathtaking natural splendor. I wasted no time in organizing a whale-watching cruise, anxious to see these amazing creatures in their natural environment. As our boat entered the broad seas of Clayoquot Sound, the suspense was obvious. The group let out a collective scream when a pod of grey whales surfaced close, their tremendous spouts shooting plumes of water into the air. It was humbling to be in the midst of such gentle giants.

The next morning, I got up early to watch the dawn at Long Beach in Pacific Rim National Park Reserve. The vast length of beach seemed to go on indefinitely, with mist-covered islets dotting the horizon. As the sun rose over the Pacific, painting the sky in pink and gold, I saw why this untamed coastline had grabbed the hearts of so many before me.

Inspired by the area's wild beauty, I decided to test myself with a journey into the jungle. The Wild Pacific Trail provided an ideal combination of ocean and woodland vistas. As I walked along the well-maintained route, the thick canopy would periodically open to expose stunning ocean views. The tremendous crash of waves against steep cliffs provided a steady backdrop for my voyage.

When I returned to Tofino, I treated myself to a gastronomic excursion at one of the town's well-known fish restaurants. The chef's tasting menu celebrated the riches of the Pacific, with each dish expressing a tale about the nearby waterways. Every taste was a celebration of Vancouver Island's culinary wonders, from flawlessly grilled scallops to delicate fish prepared using indigenous cooking traditions.

As my tour came to a conclusion, I returned to the east coast of the island, arriving in Nanaimo. I couldn't resist taking a culinary class to learn how to create the Nanaimo bar, a famous Canadian confection. Layers of chocolate, custard, and coconut were assembled under the supervision of a local pastry chef, and I left with both a new talent and a box of delights to share with friends back home.

My last day on Vancouver Island was spent discovering the underground treasures of Horne Lake Caves Provincial Park. I entered the caves with a headlamp and was accompanied by an experienced spelunker. Stalactites and stalagmites formed strange structures, while subterranean streams murmured old secrets. It was a perfect conclusion to my tour, reminding me that Vancouver Island's beauty went well beyond its surface.

As I boarded the ferry to go, I felt a combination of regret and thankfulness. Vancouver Island had revealed its various sides to me, from the elegance of Victoria to the untamed beaches of Tofino, from the depths of its caverns to the heights of its mountain paths. I had eaten its delights, inhaled its clean air, and interacted with its kind people.

The island had made an unforgettable impression on my spirit, and I knew that the memories of this vacation would inspire and renew me long after I returned home. Vancouver Island was more than simply a place; it was an experience, a journey of discovery both outside and inside. As the shoreline faded into the distance, I made a secret commitment to return, knowing that there were still endless experiences waiting for me on this magnificent island.

Brief History and Cultural Heritage

Scan QR code to see Vancouver Island

Vancouver Island's history includes a patchwork of ancient First Nations cultures, European discovery, and current Canadian identity. Long before Europeans arrived, indigenous peoples including as the Kwakwaka'wakw, Nuu-chah-nulth, and Coast Salish inhabited this island. Their rich customs, art, and strong connection to the land still affect the island's cultural environment today.

The first European to see Vancouver Island was Spanish adventurer Juan José Pérez Hernández in 1774. However, it was British Captain James Cook's visit in 1778 that sparked a surge of European interest. The island quickly became a fur trade center, with the Hudson's Bay Company erecting Fort Victoria in 1843.

As you walk through Victoria's ancient streets, you'll notice remnants of the colonial era in the majestic architecture and manicured gardens. The Parliament

Buildings, with its majestic domes and spires, reflect the island's influence on British Columbia's political scene.

But Vancouver Island's history is not limited to European settlers. The island's First Nations populations have lived here for thousands of years, their cultures inextricably linked to the land and water. Their impact may be found everywhere, from Duncan's totem poles (known as the "City of Totems") to Tofino's lively indigenous art galleries.

Speaking about art, Vancouver Island has long been a sanctuary for artists. The craggy beaches, misty woods, and varied fauna have influenced generations of painters, authors, and musicians. As you explore, you'll come across several galleries, studios, and artisan businesses displaying local talent.

The island's natural wealth has also influenced its culinary traditions. Salmon, berries, and game meats are examples of traditional First Nations foods that have impacted current island cuisine. Today, you can find this combination at farm-to-table restaurants and lively farmers' markets.

Vancouver Island's more recent history includes its participation in World War II, when it served as an important defensive position; you can still see vestiges of this era at Fort Rodd Hill National Historic Site.

As you go across the island, you'll find that each location has its own unique taste. Victoria has British charm, with its afternoon teas and double-decker buses. Up-island settlements like Tofino and Ucluelet have a more relaxed, surf-town atmosphere. The Cowichan Valley provides a unique blend of wine country and West Coast flavor.

The island's cultural legacy is very much alive and changing. Annual events such as the Victoria Symphony Splash, the Pacific Rim Whale Festival in Tofino, and the Cowichan Valley Wine Festival preserve traditions while introducing new ones.

The Royal BC Museum in Victoria is a must-see for those looking to delve deeply into the island's history. Its First Peoples Gallery provides a striking glimpse into indigenous history and culture. For a more hands-on experience, consider a guided cultural trip with a First Nations operator, where you may learn traditional weaving skills or paddle a cedar canoe.

The history of Vancouver Island is one of resilience, adaptability, and environmental stewardship. As you explore, you'll see how this distinct combination of indigenous wisdom, pioneer spirit, and modern

Canadian values has fashioned the island into the varied, dynamic destination it is today. So take your hiking boots, your desire for adventure (and seafood), and prepare to discover the various layers of Vancouver Island's intriguing history.

Geography and climate

Vancouver Island has a little bit of everything in terms of terrain and climate. Imagine you're standing on a beach, toes in the sand, gazing up at snow-capped mountains. That's Vancouver Island for you—a location where you can ski in the morning and surf in the afternoon.

This piece of land off Canada's west coast is enormous - about the size of Taiwan, if you believe it. It's long and narrow, measuring around 460 kilometers from top to bottom and 100 kilometers at its widest point. The island's backbone is a mountain range that runs through the center, with Golden Hinde, the highest peak, reaching 2,195 meters.

On the west side, you have the wild Pacific shoreline. It's rocky, dramatic, and frequently hammered by big waves—a surfer's paradise and a storm watcher's dream. The eastern side is a another story entirely. It is more protected, with calmer seas and gentler terrain. The majority of the towns and cities are located between the mountains and the sea.

Now let's speak about the weather. Vancouver Island has a reputation for being wet, and it certainly can be. But it isn't as horrible as you may imagine. Experts describe the island's climate as "temperate maritime." The Pacific Ocean acts as a large temperature regulator, resulting in warm winters and cool summers.

Here's the kicker: the island has its own microclimates. The southeast, including Victoria, is in a rain shadow. That means it's remarkably dry and sunny - far more than you'd anticipate in the Pacific Northwest. Victoria receives roughly half as much rain as Vancouver on the mainland.

When you go up to Tofino on the west coast, things change. Pacific storms hit this area hard, especially during the winter. It is not uncommon to receive more than three meters of rain per year. But don't let that deter you; those winter storms are a great magnet for visitors who come to see the massive waves crash against the coast.

The mountainous areas? They're snow magnets in the winter, which is wonderful news for skiers and boarders. Mount Washington Alpine Resort frequently has one of the thickest snowpacks in North America.

Summertime is when the island really shines. From June to September, anticipate typically dry, sunny weather with temperatures ranging from 20 to 25°C (68 to 77°F). It's ideal for hiking, camping, and visiting the beach. Just remember to bring a light jacket because evenings may become cold, even in the summer.

Keep in mind that the weather here might change quickly. You may begin your journey in sunshine and conclude it in mist. Locals will warn you to dress in layers and be prepared for rain, regardless of the weather prediction.

Spring and October are shoulder seasons, with pleasant temperatures and alternating sunny and wet days. These might be ideal seasons to come if you want to escape the summer crowds while still enjoying pleasant weather.

The geology and climate of Vancouver Island contribute significantly to its unique character. From rainforests to beaches, from foggy highlands to bright meadows, the island's numerous landscapes and weather patterns provide a playground for nature lovers and outdoor enthusiasts alike. Just remember to prepare for all seasons; you never know what Mother Nature may throw at you on this magnificent island.

When to Visit: Seasons and Events

Hello, there, fellow travelers! Thinking about when you should pack your luggage for Vancouver Island? You're in for a treat regardless of the season, so let's break it down so you can choose the best time for your island getaway.

Summer is undeniably appealing to the masses. From June to August, the island enjoys bright weather and beautiful skies. It's the perfect time to enjoy the beaches, kayak through crystal-clear seas, and soak in the laid-back island ambiance. However, this is also the time when everyone and their dog choose to pay a visit. Expect higher costs and busier areas, particularly in popular destinations like Victoria and Tokyo. If you're planning a summer vacation, make your reservations early and prepare for crowds.

Now, if you ask me, fall is something of a secret weapon. September and October are very magical months on the island. The summer crowds have thinned out, but the weather remains moderate enough for outdoor pursuits. You'll witness the woodlands turn vivid reds and golds, and there's a decent chance you'll have some of those breathtaking beaches to yourself. Plus, it's harvest season, which means wine tastings, farmer's markets, and festivals abundant.

Winter on Vancouver Island? It isn't your standard winter paradise, but it has its own appeal. From November to February, the island becomes somber and atmospheric. Storms pour in from the Pacific, creating a chaotic spectacle along the shore. It's the ideal opportunity to curl up in a cabin, drink hot chocolate, and watch the waves smash. If you enjoy watching storms, Tofino is the place to go. Just bring a decent raincoat; locals say if you don't like the weather, wait five minutes!

Spring comes in gently, yet it makes a grand arrival. From March to May, the island recovers from its winter dormancy and blooms. It's an excellent season for trekking and animal seeing; keep an eye out for migrating whales off the shore. Layers are essential because the weather might be unpredictable.

Now let's speak about events, since Vancouver Island knows how to throw a party. Victoria is a center for festivals all year. In August, don't miss the Symphony Splash, which features the Victoria Symphony performing on a floating stage in the Inner Harbour. It's just as fantastic as it sounds.

Fall brings wine and cuisine festivals. The Cowichan Valley Wine Festival in August is a must-see for wine enthusiasts, while September's Feast of Fields is a roving gourmet picnic that will make your taste buds dance.

Winter is all about enjoying the cozy sensations. Victoria's Festival of Trees in December transforms the Empress Hotel into a glittering forest, providing the ideal opportunity to indulge in their famed high tea.

Come spring, it's time for the Victoria Flower Count in March, a unique local ritual in which citizens count blossoms to show Victoria is the mildest place in Canada. It's as fantastically strange as it sounds.

The Tofino Shorebird Festival in May is a must-see for nature lovers. It's an opportunity to see thousands of migratory shorebirds and geek out with other bird enthusiasts.

Remember, every season on Vancouver Island has its own distinct taste. Whether you're looking for sun, storms, or seclusion, there's an ideal moment for your island vacation. Just be prepared to roll with the weather; it's part of the island's appeal. So, when are you planning on visiting? Trust me, whichever option you select, you're in for an incredible journey.

Chapter 1

Planning Your Trip

Getting There: Transportation Options

Vancouver Island is simple to get to, but you have choices to consider. Want to take a gorgeous boat ride? BC Ferries provides frequent service from Vancouver to Victoria and Nanaimo. It's an amazing voyage; if you're lucky, you could see orcas or sea lions. If you don't book ahead of time during peak season, you can end up waiting at the terminal.

If you have limited time, flying is a faster option. Victoria International Airport accepts flights from major Canadian and United States cities. Smaller airports in Nanaimo, Comox, and Tofino provide regional flights. Props to Harbour Air for their airplane services; landing on water is a real sensation.

Driving? The boat will also transport your wheels across. Keep in mind that island roads can be winding and narrow in areas. Take it leisurely and enjoy the scenery.

Once you're on the island, buses connect the larger settlements. Renting a car, on the other hand, will allow you to truly explore the hidden areas. Most large corporations have offices at airports and in downtown Victoria.

For the dare, why not cycle? The Galloping Goose Trail from Victoria to Sooke is beautiful. Just remember to pack your rain gear because the weather might change quickly.

Hitchhiking is legal, but use your brain. It's more typical in rural regions, so trust your instincts.

Water taxis travel between tiny islands and distant coastal areas. They're a wonderful way to explore other islands and get away from the crowds.

Regardless of how you roll, half the joy is in the trip. The island is a diversified playground, and each means of transportation provides a distinct perspective. So get your transportation and start going; Vancouver Island is waiting for you.

Visa requirements and entry regulations

Planning a visit to Vancouver Island? Before you pack your bags and plan your island itinerary, let's speak about the logistics of getting there: visas and entrance requirements.

What is the positive news? If you are a US citizen, you will not require a visa for short travels. Simply bring your passport, and you're set to go for up to six months. But don't forget that your passport should be valid for at least one day beyond your intended departure date. Trust me, you do not want to be caught at the border with an expired document.

The regulations may change somewhat for our international friends. Many tourists may require an Electronic Travel Authorization (eTA) before boarding a flight to Canada. It's a simple online form that costs only seven Canadian dollars and is generally accepted in minutes. But don't wait until the last minute; technological snags arise, so apply at least a few days before your trip.

Some passengers may require a visa, depending on their nationality and the purpose of their visit. If you want to work or study on Vancouver Island, you'll need the proper documents. The Canadian government's website provides the most up-to-date information on visa requirements.

When you arrive, be prepared to speak with a border official. They'll want to hear about your plans, including where you're staying, how long you'll be there, and maybe how much money you have to support your activities. Be honest and straightforward, and you'll be on your way to discovering Vancouver Island in no time.

One more thing: if you're bringing your pet, make sure you have their rabies vaccination certificate. Canada takes pet health seriously, and you do not want your four-legged traveling companion to be quarantined.

Remember that restrictions might change faster than the island's weather. It is generally a beneficial idea to double-check the newest criteria a few weeks before your trip. That way, you can concentrate on the enjoyable aspects, such as picking which stunning beach to visit first or which local seafood restaurant to try.

So, have you arranged your documents? Great! You're one step closer to experiencing the sea wind in your hair and the relaxed island mood in your soul. Vancouver Island awaits you, and believe me, it's worth jumping through a few administrative hoops to get there.

Budgeting for your stay on Vancouver Island might be crucial for a successful trip. This magnificent sliver of British Columbia isn't exactly inexpensive, but with some careful planning, you can enjoy its beauties without breaking the bank.

Let's start with accommodation. Your most expensive item will most likely be your bed. In high season (June to September), expect to pay between $150 and $300 CAD for a quality hotel room in popular destinations such as Victoria or Tofino. Budget vacationers, don't worry; hostels and campsites provide more affordable choices. A bed in a shared dorm may cost $30 to $50 CAD, although pitching a tent in one of the island's beautiful provincial parks often costs $15 to $35 CAD per night.

Eating out can sometimes be costly. A lunch at a modest restaurant normally costs $20 to $30 CAD per person, although nicer establishments can easily cost $50 or more. Here's a local tip: check out the food trucks and marketplaces. You'll discover delicious food that won't break the pocketbook. Another fantastic strategy to save money is to buy groceries and prepare your own meals.

Getting about the island is another consideration. Renting a car provides the most flexibility, but it comes at a cost: plan to pay $50 to $100 CAD each day, plus gas. Outside of Victoria, public transportation is less expensive but more restricted. Public transportation and taxis or ride-sharing may suffice in larger towns.

Now for the fun stuff: activities and attractions. Many of Vancouver Island's natural marvels are free to experience, such as trekking through breathtaking woods or relaxing on lovely beaches. However, some experiences cost money. Whale-watching cruises, for example, often cost $100 to $150 CAD. Museum and historical site admission fees normally vary between $15 and $25 CAD.

A sensible rule of thumb is to budget between $100 and $150 CAD each day for a reasonably comfortable trip, excluding accommodations. This should include your meals, local transportation, and a few attractions. To save money, you can live on $50 to $75 CAD per day, but you must be careful.

One more money-saving tip: timing is crucial. Visiting during the shoulder season (April-May or September-October) might get you better prices on hotels and activities. Plus, you'll avoid the summer storms.

Remember that these are approximate figures. Prices might change, particularly during peak season or for last-minute appointments. It is usually a beneficial idea to check current prices and book ahead of time if feasible. With some careful budgeting and a little flexibility, you'll discover that Vancouver Island's charm is well worth every cent.

Accommodation Options: From luxury to wilderness

Vancouver Island has a location to stay for every sort of tourist. Whether you want five-star treatment or a back-to-basics wilderness adventure, you'll find the ideal location.

Let's start with the glittery stuff. Victoria, the island's capital, is home to some extremely luxurious hotels. The Fairmont Empress is the grand dame of the group. Since 1908, this renowned château-style property has delighted guests with its waterfront views and excellent service. If you're feeling flush, rent a room in the Fairmont Gold wing, which includes access to a private lounge and concierge.

The Magnolia Hotel & Spa offers a more intimate, high-end experience. It's a short walk from the Inner Harbour and provides a boutique atmosphere with customized service. Their rooms are furnished with comfortable mattresses and huge soaking baths, ideal for relaxing after a day of touring.

If you're visiting Tofino on the wild west coast, the Wickaninnish Inn is the place to stay. Perched on a rocky ledge with spectacular ocean views, it exemplifies rustic luxury. Watch storms sweep in via your room's floor-to-ceiling windows, or visit the Ancient Cedars Spa for some real relaxation.

But Vancouver Island isn't only about luxury hotels. The island has an excellent range of comfortable bed & breakfasts that will make you feel right at home. Abbeymoore Manor in Victoria is a wonderful Edwardian mansion with tastefully designed rooms and an unforgettable breakfast. Oceanfront Grand Villa B&B in Cowichan Bay has breathtaking views of the water and the opportunity to observe seals and otters from your private terrace.

Vacation rentals are ideal for folks who like to be independent. Airbnb and VRBO provide several options around the island. You may rent everything from a luxurious downtown Victoria apartment to a remote lodge in the woods near Strathcona Provincial Park.

Speaking of cabins, if you want to experience the island wildness, you're in for a treat. Vancouver Island has some wonderful rustic lodgings that will take you right into the heart of nature. Strathcona Park Lodge provides lovely accommodations on the banks of Upper Campbell Lake. It's an excellent base for hiking, kayaking, and wildlife watching.

God's Pocket Resort on Hurst Island offers a true off-grid experience. This secluded diving resort may only be accessed by boat or floatplane. You'll stay in basic but comfortable cabins and spend your days discovering the spectacular marine life of the Broughton Archipelago.

Vancouver Island offers a plethora of camping options. The island is jam-packed with campsites, ranging from highly maintained RV parks to simple wilderness sites. Pacific Rim National Park Reserve is a popular destination, featuring camping at Green Point and Long Beach. Just make sure to reserve well in advance, since these places fill up quickly throughout the summer.

Clayoquot Wilderness Resort in Tofino offers a unique camping experience. This "glamping" resort provides luxurious tented lodgings in a secluded forest location. You'll sleep in good beds with high-thread-count sheets while still feeling connected to nature.

Budget tourists need not fear; Vancouver Island has lots of affordable choices. HI Victoria Hostel is centrally located and has both dorm and private rooms. Whalers on the Point Guesthouse in Tofino exudes a laid-back surfer feel and spectacular ocean views.

No matter where you stay on Vancouver Island, you're in for a treat. From city-center luxury to off-the-grid experiences, the island's various lodgings are an integral part of the Vancouver Island experience. So choose your ideal pad and prepare for an incredible island trip.

Chapter 2

Exploring Vancouver Island's Regions

Victoria: The Capital City

Welcome to Victoria, the pulsing heart of Vancouver Island and the capital of British Columbia. This lovely city combines old-world charm and modern flare, making it a must-see destination for every island explorer.

Walking down Government Street will make you feel as if you have gone back in time. The street's Victorian architecture is a visual feast, with intricate ironwork and colorful facades attracting your attention higher. Pop into Rogers' Chocolates for a sweet treat; they've been selling confections since 1885, and their chocolate-dipped creams are legendary.

The inner harbor is where the action happens. On bright days, the waterfront promenade is alive with excitement. Street artists go all out, delighting people with music and magic displays. Sit on a bench and watch airplanes take off and land, their propellers churning up the water as they transport people to and from Vancouver.

The Royal British Columbia Museum is a must-see for history enthusiasts. This is not your typical stuffy museum; it's a time machine. Walk through a recreated turn-of-the-century town, replete with operating stores and ambient noises that will make you forget what century you are in. The First Peoples galleries are very touching, providing detailed insights into the many traditions of British Columbia's indigenous tribes.

Hungry? Head to Fisherman's Wharf. This beautiful floating hamlet of houseboats has some of the greatest seafood restaurants in town. Grab a paper tray of fish and chips from Barb's and eat in a sunny place. Keep a lookout for the local seals, which are not bashful about begging for food.

Craigdarroch Castle is a must-see if you want to experience imperial magnificence. This Victorian-era home commemorates coal baron Robert Dunsmuir's fortune. As you climb the oak staircase and see the stained-glass windows, you'll feel as if you've stepped into the scene of a historical drama.

Butchart Gardens is a haven for gardening enthusiasts. It was once a depleted limestone quarry, but it has now transformed into a huge utopia of flowers and groomed lawns. The underground garden is especially stunning; descend into this disused quarry hole and you'll be surrounded by a riot of color and smell.

As dusk sets, head to Canada's oldest Chinatown. Fan Tan Alley, the country's smallest street, is filled with unique stores and hidden jewels. Stop by Kid Sister Ice Cream for a scoop of their ever-changing flavors—lavender honey, anyone?

For a nightcap with a view, visit the Steamship Grill & Bar. It is housed in the historic Steamship Terminal building and provides panoramic views of the bay. As dusk falls, sip on a locally produced drink while seeing the parliament buildings light up.

Victoria is considerably more than simply history and beautiful scenery. It has a young vitality, powered by the University of Victoria population. Fernwood, with its bohemian atmosphere and street art, is where the cool kids hang out. Grab a coffee at Fernwood Coffee Company and people-watch from their terrace; you could even see an impromptu street performance.

Beacon Hill Park is a must-see for outdoor enthusiasts. This large grassy spot is ideal for a morning jog or a relaxing afternoon picnic. The petting zoo is popular with children, and the high totem pole provides an excellent photo opportunity.

Victoria is a city that encourages you to slow down and enjoy the moment. Whether you're having afternoon tea at the Fairmont Empress (a long-standing tradition), kayaking in the harbor, or visiting the booths at the bustling Victoria Public Market, you'll be enchanted by this intriguing metropolis.

Cowichan Valley: Wine Country with Rural Charm

Welcome to Cowichan Valley, Vancouver Island's hidden jewel. This idyllic spot, nestled between Victoria and Nanaimo, is where the island truly shines. It's a spot where you can drink world-class wines, eat farm-fresh cuisine, and take up the laid-back rural attitude that defines Vancouver Island.

Let's discuss wine. The Cowichan Valley is not simply dabbling in viticulture; it is building a reputation for itself on a worldwide scale. Because of its distinct environment (imagine Mediterranean with a Pacific touch), this region produces some very fine wine. You'll find everything from clean whites to robust reds, as well as bubbly if you're in the mood to celebrate.

Drive down meandering rural roads, and you'll see vines dotting the slopes. Visit Blue Grouse Estate Winery for a sampling with a view; their terrace overlooks rolling hills, making you want to linger over that glass of Pinot Gris. Or visit Unsworth Vineyards, where you may enjoy your wine with a delicious meal at their on-site restaurant. Trust us, the locally sourced food is exceptional.

But Cowichan Valley is about more than simply grapes. This is a food lover's dream come true. The fertile soil and moderate temperature make it ideal for cultivating a variety of crops. You'll discover farmer's markets brimming with colorful fruit and gourmet cheeses that will make your taste buds dance, and don't get us started on seafood.

In terms of cuisine, be sure to visit Cowichan Bay village. This little seaside village is so committed to local, sustainable food that it has been classified as

North America's first Cittaslow (Slow City). Wander the boardwalk, meet friendly residents, and have a snack at one of the quaint restaurants. Rock Cod Café's fish and chips are legendary among locals.

For those who enjoy working for their food, the Cowichan Valley Trail provides 122 kilometers of picturesque hiking and biking pathways. It follows a historic railway route, so the gradients are mild, ideal for a relaxing bike or walk. You'll traverse reconstructed wooden trestles, stroll through lush woodlands, and enjoy spectacular views of the valley.

If you're up for an adventure, travel to Lake Cowichan. This enormous freshwater lake is ideal for water sports enthusiasts. Rent a kayak, try your hand at stand-up paddleboarding, or simply enjoy a refreshing swim. On hot summer days, residents like floating down the Cowichan River, so grab an inner tube and join in the fun.

As the evening approaches, consider visiting the Cowichan Performing Arts Centre in Duncan. This cutting-edge arena showcases everything from local theater plays to international music performers. It's an excellent way to wrap up a day of wine tasting and outdoor activities.

Speaking of Duncan, don't miss out on exploring this wonderful town. It is known as the "City of Totems," and it has over 40 exquisite totem poles dispersed around the urban area. Take a self-guided tour to discover the area's rich First Nations heritage.

For a really unique experience, plan your vacation around the Cowichan Valley Wine Festival in August. It's a weekend-long celebration of all things wine, complete with unique tastings, culinary pairings, and live music at vineyards around the valley.

The Cowichan Valley offers a wide selection of accommodation alternatives, from quaint B&Bs to opulent spa resorts. Stay at the Villa Eyrie Resort for a very special experience. Perched high in the Malahat Mountains, it provides amazing views of the valley and Saanich Inlet.

The Cowichan Valley is more than a place; it's an emotion. It's the feeling of slowing down and connecting with the land and the people who work it. It's about enjoying every sip of wine, mouthful of cuisine, and breathtaking vista. So come on over, relax, and let the Cowichan Valley work its magic on you. Trust us, you will not want to leave.

Nanaimo and Central Islandp

Welcome to Nanaimo and Central Vancouver Island, a pocket of paradise where urban charm meets natural majesty. This section is the island's pulsating heart, providing an ideal balance of city life and natural activities.

Nanaimo, which is often neglected by vacationers hurrying to Tofino or Victoria, is a hidden treasure just waiting to be discovered. Known as "Harbor City," it is more than just a ferry port. Stroll down the waterfront path, and you'll see why the people are so proud of their home. The busy harbor is a swarm of activity, with planes landing, boats bob in the marina, and the salty wind bringing the promise of adventure.

You can't talk about Nanaimo without mentioning its namesake treat: the Nanaimo bar. This three-layered piece of paradise is a must-try. Stop into a local bakery and grab one (or three) to fuel your adventures. If you're feeling adventurous, take a culinary class and learn how to prepare these delectable treats yourself. Trust us, your pals back home will appreciate it.

For history enthusiasts, the Nanaimo Museum is a rich mine of local legends. It's more than just dusty displays; interactive exhibits bring the city's coal mining history to life. You'll leave with a renewed respect for the tough-as-nails pioneers who formed this region.

When the sun shines (which happens more often than you think), visit Newcastle Island Marine Provincial Park. A brief boat trip from downtown, this car-free paradise is ideal for a day of hiking, swimming, or simply relaxing on the beach. Keep an eye out for the island's native raccoons; they're cunning little thieves, so guard your picnic!

Beyond Nanaimo, the center island expands like a choose-your-own-adventure novel. Parksville and Qualicum Beach, a short drive north, have some of the greatest sandy beaches on the island. At low tide, the water recedes about a kilometer, transforming the area into a huge sand and tidal pool playground. Kids (and kids at heart) will enjoy looking for sand dollars and small crabs.

For a taste of island life, take a ferry to Gabriola Island. Known as the "Isle of the Arts," it is home to a thriving community of artists and crafters. Plan your visit during the yearly studio tour to gain a behind-the-scenes glimpse at the creative process. Even if you're not an art lover, the laid-back atmosphere and breathtaking scenery are worth the trip.

Adrenaline junkies, listen up: the central island has you covered. Mount Washington Alpine Resort provides year-round excitement. In winter, cut up the slopes with breathtaking seaside vistas. In the summer, the ski runs become mountain biking paths that will put your skills to the test. If you prefer your excursions below, Horne Lake Caves Provincial Park is a subterranean paradise. Squeeze through narrow corridors, marvel at crystal formations, and immerse yourself in complete darkness; it's difficult for the faint of heart, but it's an unforgettable experience.

Foodies, you are in for a treat. The center island is a gastronomic destination, including farm-to-table restaurants, artisanal producers, and thriving marketplaces. In Nanaimo, visit the Old City Quarter for unique cafés and independent restaurants. Further out, the Cowichan Valley is becoming known as the "Napa of the North." The scenery is dotted with wineries, cideries, and farm shops, making it ideal for a gourmet road trip.

As the day comes to a close, choose a location to view the sunset. Perhaps it's from the summit of Mount Benson, with Nanaimo and the Salish Sea stretching out below. Or perhaps on a peaceful beach in Rathtrevor Provincial Park, watching the sky burst with color. Take a minute to appreciate everything, no matter where you are. This is what Vancouver Island is all about: natural beauty, friendly people, and a way of life that encourages you to slow down and enjoy the ride.

So, whether you're visiting for a weekend or a month, Nanaimo and the central island provide something for anyone. Dive in, explore, and don't be shocked if you're already planning your next visit before this one is finished. This part of Vancouver

Island has a way of capturing your heart when you least expect it.

Tofino, Ucluelet, and the wild West Coast

Welcome to Tofino, Ucluelet, and the Wild West Coast of Vancouver Island, a pocket of paradise where rough nature meets the raging Pacific. This stretch of shoreline is the stuff of surfers' and nature lovers' dreams, but don't worry if you're neither; there's something here for everyone.

Tofino, originally a small fishing community, has grown into a world-class destination while maintaining its laid-back appeal. Stroll along the main street, and you'll be divided between trendy eateries, local art galleries, and surf stores. The scent of freshly roasted coffee mingles with the salty sea air, creating a distinct Tofino vibe.

Surfing is the heartbeat of our community. Whether you're a veteran or a beginner, the beaches here feature waves for all ability levels. Chesterman Beach is a local favorite because of its large stretch of sand and regular waves. Do you have trouble distinguishing between longboards and shortboards? Don't worry. The helpful staff at the local surf schools will have you hanging ten in no time.

Tofino, however, offers more than simply surfing. Embark on a boat excursion and be ready to be astounded by the sheer magnificence of gray whales breaking the surface. If you're lucky, you may see a pod of orcas or some playful sea otter. Just remember to carry a waterproof camera; you'll want to document these memories.

As the day comes to an end, indulge yourself in some of the greatest seafood you've ever tasted. Tokyo's food scene exceeds expectations. From food trucks offering crispy fish tacos to high-end restaurants serving locally sourced delicacies, your taste buds are in for a treat.

A short journey south will take you to Ucluelet, Tofino's gentler relative. This beautiful village has a more laid-back air, if that's even conceivable in this already relaxing region of the world. The Wild Pacific Trail is a mustdo. It follows the shoreline, providing amazing vistas of the churning ocean and, if timed correctly, some of the most spectacular sunsets you'll ever see.

Visit the Ucluelet Aquarium to learn about local culture. It's modest yet teeming with intriguing aquatic life from the nearby waterways. What is the best part? After each season, all of the creatures are released back into the wild.

Now let's speak about the region's main jewel: Pacific Rim National Park Reserve. This park, situated between Tofino and Ucluelet, is Mother Nature's way of showing off. Long Beach, as its name implies, is a 16-kilometer expanse of immaculate sand and pounding waves. It's ideal for a long walk, a picnic, or simply relaxing and watching the huge waves crash in.

For a change of view, venture inland to the park's rainforest paths. The air is dense with the aroma of cedar and moss. Remember that black bears and cougars are timid but present.

Listen up, adventure seekers. Kayaking here is an unforgettable experience. Paddle around the tranquil waters of Clayoquot Sound, discovering secret coves and keeping a lookout for seals, sea lions, and bald eagles.

As darkness strikes, don't hurry inside. The stargazing here is just incredible. On a clear night, the Milky Way appears as a cosmic highway.

One piece of advice: the weather here may be unexpected. That's part of its appeal, so plan appropriately. Pack layers, a decent raincoat, and an optimistic mindset. Despite the mist and drizzle, this shoreline is eerily lovely.

Tofino, Ucluelet, and the Wild West Coast are ideal for anyone looking for adventure, leisure, or a combination of the two. It's a location that gets under your skin in the greatest way. Don't be shocked if you start arranging your return journey before you even leave.

Chapter 3

Natural Wonders and Outdoor Adventures

Pacific Rim National Park Reserve

Welcome to the wild and spectacular Pacific Rim National Park Reserve. This coastal jewel on Vancouver Island's west coast is where the forest meets the water, creating a dramatic ecological collision. It's a spot that will make you feel little in the greatest manner imaginable, with towering trees and an unending ocean.

The park is divided into three major areas: Long Beach, the Broken Group Islands, and the West Coast Trail. Each has its own flavor of adventure, so let us plunge in.

Long Beach is certainly what comes to mind when you think of "Pacific Northwest beach." It is a 16-kilometer length of beach beauty surrounded by beautiful vegetation. Surfers gather here year-round, braving the cold seas to catch some of Canada's greatest waves. If you're new to surfing, don't worry; there are several surf schools in neighboring Tofino that will have you hanging ten in no time.

For those who like to keep their feet on firm ground, the beach is ideal for lengthy walks, beachcombing, or simply resting and watching the huge Pacific waves crash in. Keep a watch out for bald eagles flying above, as well as the odd black bear ambling down the coastline during low tide.

The Broken Group Islands are a kayakers's paradise. This archipelago of over 100 tiny islands and islets can only be reached by boat, making it feel like your own little paradise. Paddle across crystal-clear seas, camp on quiet beaches, and witness some of the most breathtaking sunrises you've ever seen. Just remember to reserve your camping permits in advance; this location is popular for a reason.

If you're looking for a true challenge, the West Coast Trail awaits. This 75-kilometer trekking path is not for the faint-hearted. It's a muddy, rooty, ladder-climbing experience that will push your limits while rewarding you with breathtaking coastline vistas. Plan on taking roughly a week to complete the path and be prepared for any weather conditions; after all, this is the rainforest.

However, Pacific Rim is more than just a series of thrilling experiences. The park is a biodiversity hotspot, with innumerable plant and animal species. Take a trip along the Rainforest Trail, a boardwalk that snakes among ancient cedars and hemlocks dripping with moss. It's like strolling through Nature's Cathedral.

To see some of the park's aquatic fauna, go to the Kwisitis Visitor Center. During the migration season, you may observe gray whales spouting offshore from its deck. If you're lucky, you could see sea lions, harbor seals, and even the rare orca.

When it comes to animals, remember that you are in their land. Keep your food sealed and well kept, particularly if you're camping. Nobody wants a hungry grizzly or a smart raccoon to pay them a visit at midnight.

The park's rich First Nations heritage offers additional dimension to your experience. The Nuu-chah-nulth people have lived in this area for thousands of years, and their culture is strongly rooted in the land and water. Take the time to learn about their customs and history; you'll have a whole new appreciation for this remarkable location.

Before you leave, stop by the Pacific Rim Visitor Center at the park entrance. The staff can provide you with up-to-date information on trail conditions, wildlife sightings, and tide tables, which is essential if you plan any beach activities.

Remember that the weather here may change in a flash. One minute you're enjoying the sun, the next you're in the midst of a foggy rainstorm. Pack clothes, pack rain gear, and accept the unexpected; it's all part of the Pacific Rim experience.

Whether you're surfing, hiking, kayaking, or simply taking in the raw beauty of this coastal wilderness, Pacific Rim National Park Reserve will be with you long after you leave. It's more than simply a park; it serves as a reminder of the natural world's strength and beauty, as well as our little but vital role in it.

Strathcona Provincial Park

Welcome to Strathcona Provincial Park, the treasure of Vancouver Island's wildness. This vast stretch of rocky mountains, clear lakes, and old forests is a playground for both outdoor enthusiasts and environment lovers.

Strathcona is the oldest provincial park in British Columbia, having been established in 1911. It's a location where time seems to stand still, with landscapes that have mainly stayed untouched throughout millennia. As you travel through the park's meandering roads, you'll feel the outer world fade away, overwhelmed with amazement at the sheer magnificence of the scenery.

The park's main attraction is Buttle Lake, a long, fjord-like body of water that, on calm days, reflects the surrounding peaks like a mirror. It's an ideal camping location, with numerous well-kept campsites dotting its shoreline. Wake up to the sound of loons singing across the river and the aroma of cedar in the air—there's no better way to start the day in Strathcona.

The park is a hiker's paradise. Trails range from pleasant family hikes to difficult wilderness excursions that will challenge even the most experienced hikers. The Elk River Trail is a popular route, traveling through old-growth forests before opening out to spectacular alpine meadows. If you're looking for a true adventure, try the multi-day walk to the top of Golden Hinde, Vancouver Island's highest mountain. Just remember to bring lots of water and food; the vistas from the summit are worth every step.

Strathcona has something to offer water lovers as well. Buttle Lake and its neighbor, Upper Campbell Lake, provide great swimming, fishing, and boating conditions. Rent a canoe or kayak and paddle down the coast, keeping an eye out for bald eagles flying overhead and black bears grazing on the banks.

Winter turns Strathcona into a beautiful paradise. Mount Washington Alpine Resort, located just outside the park limits, is a popular skiing and snowboarding destination. If you prefer a calmer winter experience, put on some snowshoes and explore the park's pathways in their frozen state. The stillness of a snowcovered woodland is quite unique.

Della Falls, one of Canada's tallest waterfalls, is a hidden beauty in Strathcona. It's not simple to get to—you'll have to take a boat across Great Central Lake and then climb for several hours—but the sight of water flowing down a 440-meter rock face is breathtaking.

Wildlife viewing is another attraction of any trip to Strathcona. The park is home to a broad range of species, including tiny Vancouver Island marmots (one of North America's rarest mammals) and stately Roosevelt elk. Keep your eyes peeled and your camera ready; you never know what you'll see.

Before you go, stop at the Strathcona Park Wilderness Centre in the adjacent town of Gold River. The courteous staff can give current information on trail conditions, wildlife sightings, and park cautions. They also provide interpretative programs to help you better understand and appreciate this wonderful location.

One word of caution: Strathcona's beauty is only equaled by its isolation. Cell phone reception is patchy at best, and facilities in the area are scarce. Come prepared with lots of supplies, a decent map, and a healthy appreciation for nature. Also, always inform someone of your plans before setting out on the path.

Strathcona Provincial Park is more than a destination; it is an experience. Whether you're looking for adventure, solitude, or just a chance to reconnect with nature, you'll find it here. So put up your hiking boots, take a deep breath of the fresh mountain air, and prepare to make some amazing memories in one of Vancouver Island's most stunning natural treasures.

Whalewatching and Marine Life

Grab your binoculars and get ready for a breathtaking show off the coast of Vancouver Island. This part of British Columbia offers some of the greatest whale viewing on the globe. It's difficult to imagine a more exhilarating way to spend a day than bobbing on the waves, searching the horizon for telltale spouts.

From March to October, the waterways surrounding Vancouver Island become a busy marine highway. Gray whales lead the assault, traveling north from Mexico to Alaska. These gentle giants, which may exceed 45 feet in length, frequently approach the shore, providing lucky beachgoers with a free performance.

But who are the true stars of the show? Orcas. These black-and-white beauties live in these waters year-round. You could see a pod of resident orcas pursuing salmon, or, if you're lucky, a group of transient orcas looking for seals or sea lions. Keep a watch out for their unmistakable dorsal fins slashing through the waves.

Between June and September, humpback whales take center stage. These acrobatic giants like putting on a show, bursting out of the water, and slapping their gigantic pectorals. It's a sight that will make you slack-jawed and reach for your camera.

Don't ignore the supporting characters, though. Minke whales, although being smaller and more elusive, make regular sightings. And don't forget the fun Dall's and harbor porpoises, who are frequently seen dashing alongside tour boats.

When it comes to tours, you have plenty of possibilities. For an adrenaline-pumping trip, board a quick zodiac, or if you're concerned about sea legs, choose a more stable catamaran. Many cruises depart from Victoria's Inner Harbour, while Tofino and Telegraph Cove on the island's wilder west coast provide a more adventurous experience.

Pro tip: Schedule your tour early in your trip. If the weather doesn't cooperate, most businesses will allow you to reschedule. Don't forget to dress in layers since it may be chilly out on the ocean, even in the summer.

While whales may be the stars, the supporting cast is as remarkable. Keep a watch out for bald eagles swooping overhead, with their distinctive white heads easily visible against the blue sky. Seals and sea lions frequently recline on rocky ledges, barking up a storm when vessels pass.

Telegraph Cove in August offers a genuinely memorable experience. You may kayak alongside orcas as they massage themselves on smooth pebble beaches, a habit peculiar to this group of whales.

Remember, these are wild creatures in their natural environment. While sightings are regular, they are not guaranteed. On the sea, you never know what you'll see, which is exciting.

After your whale-watching trip, visit Sidney's Shaw Centre for the Salish Sea to learn more about marine life. This hands-on aquarium exhibits the remarkable diversity of the surrounding waterways. Both kids and adults love the touch pools, where you can interact with the animals.

The seas around Vancouver Island are teeming with life, from the smallest plankton to the largest whales. A whale-watching excursion here is more than just a tourist pastime; it's a front-row ticket to one of nature's most spectacular displays. So come on; the whales are waiting.

Hiking, camping, and eco-tourism opportunities

Vancouver Island's wild heart invites both adventurers and nature lovers. From misty rainforests to craggy coasts, this Pacific Northwest treasure is a playground for hikers, campers, and eco-tourists of all kinds.

Lace up your boots and hit the trails—Vancouver Island has treks for all skill levels. Beginners may stretch their legs on the simple Juan de Fuca Trail in Sooke, which winds along beaches and through beautiful forests. The West Coast Trail is a true challenge. This 75-kilometer walk is not for the faint of heart, but the rewards are well worth it: gorgeous beaches, secret waterfalls, and the opportunity to see whales breaching offshore.

Don't miss Strathcona Provincial Park, the island's oldest and largest. The Forbidden Plateau is a hiker's dream, with routes winding through alpine meadows filled with crystal-clear lakes. Keep an eye out for black bears and Roosevelt elk wandering the forest.

Camping offers a wide range of options. Beachgoers will enjoy pitching their tents at Pachena Bay Campground in Bamfield. Fall asleep to the sound of waves and awaken to stunning ocean vistas. For a more rural experience, travel inland to Buttle Lake in Strathcona Park. Surrounded by towering mountains and old-growth woods, it's the ideal starting point for discovering the park's hidden beauties.

Eco-tourism is thriving on Vancouver Island, with several opportunities to get up close and personal with nature while treading lightly. Kayak trips in Clayoquot Sound provide an opportunity to kayak among sea otters and harbor seals. Join a whale watching excursion at Telegraph Cove to see orcas and humpback whales in the Johnstone Strait's nutrient-rich waters.

Staying in one of the island's eco-lodges will provide you with an amazing experience. The Wildside Guesthouse near Tofino is located on the border of the Clayoquot Sound UNESCO Biosphere Reserve. You may explore old-growth woods, learn about local ecology, and even participate in active conservation efforts.

Hikers should not pass up Cape Scott Provincial Park on the island's northern point. The Cape Scott Trail offers a hearty dose of harsh coastal scenery, including white-sand beaches, wind-swept headlands, and the opportunity to see bald eagles soar overhead. Just prepare for a lot of muck.

If you don't have much time but still want to be outside, visit East Sooke Regional Park. The Coast

Trail here delivers a punch, with breathtaking ocean views, secluded coves, and petroglyphs left by the area's First Nations inhabitants. It's an ideal day excursion from Victoria.

The North Island's karst landscapes provide a unique eco-adventure experience. These limestone structures generate unearthly caverns and sinkholes. Join a guided tour of the Horne Lake Caves to navigate narrow corridors and wonder at underground waterfalls.

Don't forget to review your Leave No Trace guidelines before venturing out. Because Vancouver Island's ecosystems are fragile, we must keep them clean for future generations. Pack out what you bring in, stay on designated pathways, and allow wildlife plenty of space.

Whether you're an experienced backpacker or a first-time camper, Vancouver Island's natural beauties will astound you. So gather your supplies, fill your water bottle, and prepare for the experience of a lifetime.

Chapter 4

Cultural Experiences and First Nations Heritage

Indigenous Art and Traditions

The bright heartbeat of Indigenous art and customs can be felt all throughout Vancouver Island. This isn't your typical tourist trap; it's a live, breathing display of tribes who have inhabited this region for millennia.

Take a trip around downtown Victoria, and you will come across Thunderbird Park. It's more than simply a park; it's an open-air gallery with towering totem poles pointing to the sky, each presenting a story passed down through generations. You could see a professional carver at work, their hands expertly molding cedar into exquisite shapes. Don't be bashful; most artists are glad to talk about their work if you express real curiosity.

Visit the Royal BC Museum to learn more about Indigenous art. Their First Peoples Gallery is a rich collection of antiquities and modern pieces. You'll see everything from delicately woven baskets to massive houseposts. The museum frequently offers special exhibitions, so check the schedule; you could be lucky enough to see a presentation exhibiting emerging Indigenous artists.

But Vancouver Island's Indigenous art culture isn't limited to museums. Head over to Alert Bay on Cormorant Island to immerse yourself in the Kwakwaka'wakw culture. The U'mista Cultural Center is a must-see. It houses a collection of potlatch regalia that was previously taken by the government but has since been returned to its rightful owners. The masks and ceremonial artifacts displayed here are not only gorgeous but also potent symbols of cultural persistence.

If you're in Nanaimo, visit the Nanaimo Art Gallery. They routinely host shows by Indigenous artists who combine traditional techniques with contemporary themes. It's an excellent spot to observe how old art forms have evolved in the modern world.

For those prepared to step off the main road, the secluded community of Kyuquot provides a one-of-a-kind experience. Here, you can witness Nuu-chah-nulth craftsmen make beautiful silver and gold jewelry, frequently blending traditional motifs into modern pieces. If you're lucky, you might be able to join in a workshop and create your own artwork.

However, Indigenous traditions on Vancouver Island encompass more than just visual art. Music and dance have a significant cultural impact. If you time your visit correctly, you might be able to catch the Tribal Journeys, an annual event in which First Nations from all across the Pacific Northwest journey in traditional canoes, ending in days of celebration, storytelling, and performance.

Food is another method to immerse yourself in Indigenous cultures. In Victoria, keep a lookout for the Songhees Seafood and Steam food truck. They provide traditional Coast Salish food with a contemporary touch. Think wild fish burgers and bannock tacos; it's a delightful way to experience the delicacies that have supported people here for millennia.

For a more immersive experience, consider staying at Wya Point Resort in Ucluelet. The Yuułuʔiłʔatḥ First Nation owns and operates the lodges, which provide comfortable accommodations. But the true lure is their cultural trips, which include learning about traditional plant usage, weaving, and listening to stories around a beach bonfire.

Remember that Indigenous art and customs on Vancouver Island are not relics of the past; they are active, developing activities. Respect is essential. Always obtain permission before shooting artists or their work, and be careful of sensitive locations and ceremonies.

As you explore, you'll discover that Vancouver Island's Indigenous art and customs are more than simply sights to see; they're experiences that will stay with you long after you leave the island. Each sculpture, song, and tale contributes to the complex tapestry of civilizations that have formed this wonderful part of the globe.

Museums and Historic Sites

The museums and historical monuments on Vancouver Island are a must-see for both history aficionados and cultural vultures. As you explore these intriguing locations, you'll feel as if you've stepped back in time.

Let's start with the Royal BC Museum in Victoria. This location is quite popular, and for excellent reason. It's not your typical museum; it's more like a time machine. One minute you're wandering through a reconstructed Victorian street, full with era-appropriate noises and scents, and the next you're face-to-face with a woolly mammoth. The First Peoples Gallery is a must-see for those interested in the rich cultural legacy of British Columbia's indigenous peoples.

Craigdarroch Castle is only a stone's throw away. This Victorian-era home reflects the opulence of coal tycoon Robert Dunsmuir. As you ascend the creaking stairs and peer into beautifully painted apartments, you can almost hear the murmurs of high society gossip from a century ago. The stained-glass windows are especially beautiful; on a sunny day, they cast vibrant patterns on the antique furnishings.

For a flavor of military history, visit Fort Rodd Hill and Fisgard Lighthouse National Historic Sites. These coastal defensive structures provide insight into Canada's maritime history. Kids (and large kids at heart) will enjoy exploring the subterranean magazines and weaponry. The lighthouse, built on a rocky cliff, is exceptionally attractive; prepare your camera.

Up in Nanaimo, the Nanaimo Museum delves into the city's coal mining history. It's not all dark tunnels and pickaxes, though; you'll also learn about the city's unusual relationship to the popular Nanaimo bar. Yes, there's a whole museum dedicated to a dessert!

The Vancouver Island Military Museum offers a more solemn, but equally essential, historical experience. It's modest, yet it's packed with relics from both World Wars. The personal experiences of Vancouver Island veterans vividly illustrate the impact of global conflicts in local communities.

If you find yourself in the Comox Valley, be sure to visit the Courtenay & District Museum and Palaeontology Centre. It may sound like a mouthful, but believe me, it's worth a visit. The main attraction here is the Elasmosaur, an 80-million-year-old marine monster unearthed on Vancouver Island. You may also take a fossil tour and try to locate your own ancient keepsake.

For a taste of nautical history, visit the nautical museum of British Columbia in Victoria. From First Nations canoes to current cargo ships, this museum depicts the province's close link with the water. The model ship collection is very outstanding, with precise features that will astound you.

Finally, go to Duncan to explore the Cowichan Valley Museum. This attractive museum, located in a disused railway station, presents the narrative of the region's different populations. From early settlers to Cowichan peoples, you'll get a true feel of the valley's unique cultural tapestry.

Remember that these museums and historical places are more than simply dusty old buildings packed with stuff. They serve as historical gateways, providing insight into the people and events that formed Vancouver Island. So push open those creaking doors and immerse yourself in the island's rich past. Who knows what mysteries you may uncover?

Festivals and cultural events

The festival scene on Vancouver Island is a year-round party to remember. From toe-tapping music to mouthwatering culinary festivals, there's always something going on in this Pacific paradise.

At the Laketown Shakedown, you may dance in the sand without wearing shoes. This summer music festival in Cowichan Valley combines big names and local talent for three days of rock, hip-hop, and everything in between. Pack your sunscreen and prepare to party under the warm island sun.

Do you have a sweet tooth? The Nanaimo Bar Festival is your passport to sweet joy. This unique event honors the popular Canadian dessert with baking competitions, tastings, and even a Nanaimo bar-themed obstacle course. You'll leave with a sugar rush and a newfound respect for this three-layered treat.

Every February, the Victoria Film Festival puts out the red carpet for moviegoers. Discover independent films, documentaries, and shorts from across the world. Rub elbows with filmmakers during Q&A sessions and after-parties; who knows, you could see the next amazing thing in cinema.

The Cowichan Valley Wine Festival takes place each fall. Sip your way around the region's vineyards, meeting enthusiastic winemakers and discovering new favorites. With breathtaking valley vistas as your backdrop, it's the ideal way to celebrate the harvest season.

Art enthusiasts, mark your calendars for the Sooke Fine Arts Show. This 11-day festival features the finest of Vancouver Island's artistic skills. From paintings to sculptures, it's a visual feast and an opportunity to bring home a one-of-a-kind gift.

The Victoria Highland Games & Celtic Festival is a must-see for those interested in island history. Traditional Scottish sports have kilts swirling and bagpipes screaming as contestants face off. Grab a meal of haggis (if you dare) and cheer on the caber tossers—it's a wild party, even if you don't have a drop of Scottish blood.

Listen up, foodies: the Feast of Fields is your chance to enjoy the island's wealth. This roaming gourmet picnic connects local chefs with farmers and suppliers. Stroll around the orchards and fields, snacking on farm-fresh fare and enjoying Island-made wines and ciders. This is a locavore's dream come true.

When winter arrives, Victoria celebrates with the Magic of Christmas celebration. The Inner Harbour becomes a glittering wonderland, filled with carol performers, holiday markets, and horse-drawn carriage rides. It's the perfect remedy for those short, dreary days.

The Pulling Together Canoe Journey in Port Alberni provides an opportunity to learn about Indigenous culture. First Nations communities from throughout the area come together for this spectacular celebration of culture and solidarity. Watch hand-carved boats sail across the lake and participate in feasts and storytelling sessions on shore.

Finally, the Vancouver Island MusicFest in the Comox Valley is a summer highlight. This varied event features many stages and camping options, spanning styles from folk to funk. Bring your dancing shoes and an open mind; you're sure to find your new favorite band.

Regardless of when you arrive, Vancouver Island's festival schedule ensures a wonderful time. These events are more than simply tourist attractions; they offer a glimpse into the heart and spirit of island life. So dig in, talk to the people, and make some amazing experiences. After all, that is the point of travel, right?

Art galleries and local crafts

The art culture on Vancouver Island is both visually and spiritually stimulating. From First Nations treasures to modern works, you'll be blown away by the talent on show. Let's start with a visit to the Art Gallery of Greater Victoria. This institution is a true gem, nestled in a stunning home that is worth seeing on its own. Inside, you'll find an eclectic mix of

Asian art, Emily Carr paintings, and rotating exhibits that will have you returning for more.

If you're in Nanaimo, be sure to visit the Nanaimo Art Gallery. It's a tiny venue with a strong focus on local and Canadian artists. The gallery frequently organizes participatory classes, so you may leave with a new talent under your belt.

For a more personal encounter, visit the Comox Valley Art Gallery in Courtenay. This community-driven facility features the finest of Vancouver Island's artistic talent. You'll often see the artists themselves lingering around, eager to discuss their work.

Now, let us discuss local crafts. Vancouver Island is a hotspot for handcrafted ingenuity. In Victoria, the Craft Council of British Columbia Gallery is your one-stop shop for handcrafted items. From delicate jewelry to unusual pottery, you'll discover something one-of-a-kind to take home.

Chemainus offers a real Vancouver Island craft experience. This little town is well-known for its murals, but it also has some excellent artisan businesses. The Chemainus Public Market is an excellent location to start. Hand-carved wooden bowls, locally manufactured soaps, and candles are among the items available.

If you're looking for a picturesque drive, go to Tofino. This surf town boasts a vibrant artistic culture. The Roy Henry Vickers Gallery features magnificent prints inspired by First Nations culture and the harsh West Coast terrain. Just down the road is the House of Himwitsa Native Art Gallery, which showcases beautiful carvings, jewelry, and textiles created by local Indigenous artists.

Don't overlook the hidden delights in little villages. Salt Spring Island, a short boat trip from Vancouver Island, is an artists' haven. The Saturday Market in Ganges is a sensory overload of local items, ranging from tie-dyed t-shirts to handcrafted ceramics.

Visit Comox during the Filberg Festival for a genuinely one-of-a-kind experience. This yearly festival brings together more than 100 craftspeople from throughout the province. It's an excellent opportunity to observe demonstrations, speak with crafters, and purchase one-of-a-kind items.

If you enjoy textile arts, visit the Maiwa Handprints business in Nanaimo. This location is a treasure trove of organically dyed fabrics, handcrafted textiles, and lovely clothes. They frequently organize workshops, so you may find yourself learning how to indigo dye or weave on a backstrap loom.

The art galleries and artisan businesses on Vancouver Island are more than simply shopping destinations; they are windows into the island's character. Each item conveys a tale about the land, the people, and the diverse cultural fabric that makes this region so unique. So take your time, talk to the artists and store owners, and be amazed by the amazing talent everywhere.

Remember that art is omnipresent on Vancouver Island. Keep a lookout for public sculptures, street art, and temporary exhibitions in cafés and restaurants. You never know where you'll discover your next favorite piece.

Chapter 5

Culinary Delights of Vancouver Island

Farm-to-table experiences

Vancouver Island's farm-to-table scene is a foodie's dream. This sliver of paradise off Canada's west coast is more than simply breathtaking scenery; it's also a hotspot of culinary ingenuity, with chefs and farmers working together to deliver the freshest tastes to your plate.

Take a trip in the Cowichan Valley, and you'll come across a mosaic of small farms, orchards, and vineyards. Growers in this region benefit from the moderate environment, which allows them to plant anything from delicious berries to crisp greens almost all year. Visit one of the numerous farm stalls dotting the countryside, and you could find yourself conversing with the farmer who harvested your vegetables that morning.

For a hands-on experience, visit Healing Farm on the Saanich Peninsula. They provide classes where you can get your hands dirty and learn about sustainable agricultural methods. After working up an appetite in the fields, you'll sit down to a lunch made using the ingredients you just picked. It's a pure farm-to-table experience.

In Victoria, the farm-to-table movement is thriving. Restaurants like 10 Acres Bistro embrace the notion, getting the majority of their food from their own farm just outside the city. Take a seat on their terrace and enjoy meals that highlight the island's wealth, such as a vibrant heirloom tomato salad or a flawlessly grilled fillet of locally caught fish.

Don't pass up the opportunity to explore the busy Victoria Public Market. This food lover's utopia unites local farmers, bakers, and craftsmen under one roof. Strike up a discussion with sellers about their goods, and you can leave with not just a bag full of delights but also a piece of local culinary history.

The Comox Valley has a vibrant community of organic growers and food entrepreneurs. The Locals Restaurant in Courtenay stands out, with a menu that reads like a who's who of local suppliers. Chef Ronald St. Pierre's creations are a love letter to Vancouver Island's terroir, evolving with the seasons and never disappointing.

Join Island Tides & Bites for a unique farm-to-table experience. You'll be cruising the seas off Quadra Island, learning about sustainable aquaculture and enjoying freshly picked oysters and other seafood treats. It reminds us that on Vancouver Island, the "farm" spreads into the surrounding oceans.

Back on land, the annual Feast of Fields festival is a must-see for any foodie. This traveling gourmet picnic takes place at a new farm each year, bringing together the island's best chefs, farmers, fishers, and food artisans. It's a celebration of local cuisines and an opportunity to meet the people behind the food.

As you tour Vancouver Island's farm-to-table scene, you'll discover a common thread: a profound appreciation for the land and sea that give so much abundance. Knowing your food's origins and effort is as important as eating healthy.

So, the next time you visit Vancouver Island, avoid commercial eateries and instead explore the local cuisine scene. Whether you're picking berries fresh from the bush, shucking oysters by the coast, or dining at a restaurant where the chef knows every farmer by name, you're in for a treat. This is more than simply eating; it's a delectable trip through the heart and soul of Vancouver Island.

Seafood specialties and where to find them

Vancouver Island has an incredible seafood scene. From little coastal shacks to fancy restaurants, you're never far from a dish of ocean-fresh delight. Let's look at the island's greatest catches and where to locate them.

First up: salmon. It's the Pacific Northwest's most common fish. But for a true treat, visit Sooke Harbour House. This tiny eatery serves wild-caught salmon that will have you wondering why you ever bothered with farmed salmon. Their cedar-planked salmon is a local favorite, smokey, tender, and packed with flavor.

Are you craving shellfish? Fanny Bay is your go-to. This little village is an oyster center, and the Fanny Bay Inn serves them in bucketloads. Slurp them raw or grilled with garlic butter. Either way, you're in for a salty treat.

Now, let us discuss spot prawns. These lovely tiny crustaceans are a Vancouver Island delicacy, and they are only available for a few weeks each spring. If you're lucky enough to come during spotprawn season, head straight to the Wickaninnish Inn in Tofino. Their spot-prawn risotto is the stuff of fantasies.

Red Fish Blue Fish in Victoria offers a more informal atmosphere. This waterfront food truck delivers fish and chips that will spoil you for all others. Their halibut is crispy on the exterior, flaky on the inside, and served with hand-cut fries that are dangerously irresistible.

Listen up, crab lovers. The Crab Lady in Cowichan Bay is a must-see. It's not spectacular, just a little stand on the wharf, but the Dungeness crab is as fresh as it comes. Crack open a whole crab with a view of the bay, and you'll understand why locals recommend this eatery.

If you're looking for something more exotic, try the octopus at Pluvio in Ucluelet. This premium restaurant transforms the often-chewy mollusk into a soft, delicious dish that might be the highlight of your visit.

Don't forget the simple fish taco. Tacofino, which began as a food truck in Tofino and now has outlets around the island, provides crispy fish tacos worth traveling for. Combine them with a local craft beer for the whole Vancouver Island experience.

Tofino's Wolf in the Fog offers a real farm-to-table (or should we say sea-to-table) experience. Their menu changes with the seasons and the catch, but you can always expect inventive dishes with the finest of local seafood.

Last but not least, let's discuss fish and chips. You can't throw a stone on Vancouver Island without hitting a fish and chip store, but for something unique, visit Jigger's in Nanoose Bay. Their secret batter recipe has been attracting customers for decades.

Remember that Vancouver Island is all about fresh, sustainable seafood. Most restaurants take pleasure in sourcing locally and sustainably. So don't be shy: ask your server where the fish originated from. You could discover something new about the island's fishing economy.

Here's a pro tip: if you're feeling daring, book one of the island's many fishing trips. There is nothing quite like catching your own meal. Many local eateries will prepare your catch for you.

From high-end restaurants to simple food trucks, Vancouver Island's seafood sector has something for everyone's taste and budget. So, loosen your belt and prepare to eat your way around the island. Believe me, your taste buds will appreciate you.
wineries, breweries, and distilleries

Liquid gold on Vancouver Island: wineries, breweries, and distilleries

Grab your glass and prepare for a tipsy tour of Vancouver Island's top drinking establishments. This sliver of Pacific paradise is more than simply breathtaking scenery; it's also a drinker's dream. From sun-soaked wineries to hop-happy breweries and small-batch spirit manufacturers, the island has something to whet every appetite.

Let's start with the wine scene. The Cowichan Valley, known as "Canada's Provence," is where the magic happens. Thanks to its Mediterranean-like atmosphere, this region produces some pretty fine wine. Blue Grouse Estate Winery is a must-visit. Their tasting facility has stunning views of the vineyards, and their Ortega white is a popular favorite—smooth, fragrant, and ideal for a sunny afternoon.

If you want something more daring, go to Unsworth Vineyards. Their Pinot Noir is the highlight of the show, with cherry aromas and a dash of spice. The on-site restaurant is an excellent place to refuel between tastings.

Now for the beer. Victoria, the island's capital, is a hopper's paradise. Phillips Brewing & Malting Co. is a local institution. Their Blue Buck Ale is essentially the unofficial beer of Vancouver Island; sample it and you'll understand why. For something a little different, visit Driftwood Brewery. Their Fat Tug IPA is a hop explosion that will blow your socks off.

If you find yourself in Comox, don't miss out on Land & Sea Brewing Company. Their Glacier Cream Ale is smooth, simple to drink, and dangerously moreish. The taproom also has a terrific feel, making it ideal for sharing travel stories with locals and fellow travelers.

Let's move on to more difficult topics. Craft distilleries are popping up across the island, making great spirits. Sheringham Distillery in Sooke is leading the way. Their Seaside Gin, made from local flying kelp, has received worldwide accolades. It creates a unique G&T experience.

Wayward Distillation House in the Comox Valley is taking a unique approach. They utilize honey as the foundation for all of their spirits, producing exceptionally smooth and tasty mixtures. Their Krupnik, a spiced honey liqueur, tastes like Christmas in a glass.

For whisky enthusiasts, Shelter Point Distillery near Campbell River is the place to go. Their single malt whiskey, distilled from barley cultivated on their seaside farm, rivals certain Scottish whiskies.

Driving between these locations might be hard, especially after a few tastings. Consider taking a guided tour or appointing a driver. Many destinations also have lodgings, allowing you to truly relax and enjoy yourself.

Also, it's about the stories that go with the drinks. Talk to the artists, learn about their work, and enjoy each drink from the heart. Whether you're a serious aficionado or just like the odd drink, Vancouver Island's drink culture will leave you in excellent spirits.

Food festivals and culinary tours

The food culture on Vancouver Island is a feast for the senses, and there's no better way to get started than with one of its exciting food festivals or gourmet excursions. From farm-fresh fruit to ocean-to-table seafood, this island paradise offers a plethora of tastes to make your taste buds dance.

Let's start with the Feast of Fields, a traveling gourmet harvest celebration where you'll graze your way across local farms. Picture this: You're wandering through sun-dappled orchards, eating dishes prepared by famous chefs with ingredients sourced from the exact land you stand on. It's a hands-on, muddy boots type of experience that ties you directly to the island's agricultural heritage.

If you enjoy seafood, don't miss the BC Seafood Festival in the Comox Valley. This seafaring feast is a shellfish enthusiast's dream come true. You'll suck oysters, eat luscious crab legs, and perhaps even participate in shucking competitions. What is the best part? You'll be rubbing shoulders with local fishermen who will regale you with salty stories about life on the sea.

The Cowichan Valley Wine Festival transforms wine tasting into a fascinating treasure hunt for people who enjoy a little competitiveness with their cuisine. With a map and a wine glass, you'll fly between vineyards, enjoying crisp whites and strong reds while taking in the breathtaking valley vistas. It's like a treasure quest, except instead of riches, you're looking for the ideal Pinot Noir.

Now, let us discuss culinary tours. Tofino food tours are essential for any serious foodie. You'll explore this surf town's diverse culinary culture, which includes everything from hidden gem food trucks to high-end eateries. One minute you're eating freshly caught fish tacos, and the next you're learning how to make the ideal Caesar cocktail (Canada's zestier version of the Bloody Mary).

A First Nations culinary tour provides an in-depth look at the island's unique food. You could find yourself searching for traditional ingredients in verdant woodlands or studying ancient culinary skills on the seashore. It's an effective approach to connecting with the land's rich cultural past via your taste sensations.

Do not feel left out, beer aficionados. Victoria Beer Week is a sudsy festival that will have you jumping between breweries quicker than you can say "IPA." From sour beer lectures to food and beer pairing dinners, this crash course in craft brewing will transform you into a true beer snob (in the nicest way possible).

Roll up your sleeves and sign up for a culinary lesson at The London Chef in Victoria. You can prepare a West Coast seafood feast or learn how to make artisanal bread. What is the best part? You get to consume your masterpieces later, coupled with local wines, of course.

And here's a little secret: Keep an eye out for pop-up farm meals. These under-the-radar gatherings frequently feature guest chefs cooking multi-course dinners in the midst of scenic farmland. It's like discovering a hidden supper club, with each meal telling a narrative about the surrounding landscape.

Food festivals and culinary excursions on Vancouver Island are more than simply an opportunity to eat; they are sensory experiences. You will meet enthusiastic food producers, learn about sustainable techniques, and develop a better understanding of the island's gastronomic legacy. So come hungry, curious, and ready for a culinary adventure that will stay with you long after you've cleaned your plate clean.

Chapter 6

Urban Exploration and Shopping

Victoria's Inner Harbour and Downtown

Welcome to Victoria's Inner Harbour and Downtown, the vibrant hub of British Columbia's capital city. This waterfront wonderland combines history and contemporary, providing a dynamic combination of sights, sounds, and flavors that will keep you entertained from sunrise until nightfall.

Start your day with a stroll through the lively Inner Harbour. It's a swarm of activity from the start, with float planes landing on the water and water taxis zooming across the bay. Grab a coffee from one of the neighborhood cafés and watch the city awaken.

You can even see street artists preparing their shows for the day.

The Parliament Buildings are without a doubt the harbor's crown gem. These massive, neo-baroque monuments are a photographer's dream, especially when illuminated at night. Come in for a free tour and learn everything about British Columbia's political environment. The Royal BC Museum, located across the street, is a treasure mine of nature and human history. Their First Peoples collection is especially fascinating, providing detailed insights into the province's indigenous customs.

Do you fancy some afternoon tea? The Fairmont Empress Hotel is the place to be. This ivy-covered grand dame has been serving scones and finger sandwiches for almost a century. It's expensive, but when in Victoria, right?

As you go around downtown, you'll come across Chinatown, the second oldest in Canada behind San Francisco. Duck into Fan Tan Alley, the country's tiniest street. It's dotted with unique stores and restaurants that will make you feel like you've entered another universe.

Hungry? Head to the Victoria Public Market on the Hudson. This gourmet paradise features the finest of Vancouver Island's agriculture. For a taste of local comfort cuisine, head to the famed Saltchuk Pie Company.

Beacon Hill Park is your go-to spot for some green in the city. It's only a short walk from downtown and ideal for a picnic or a relaxing afternoon. Keep a watch out for peacocks strutting their thing, since they control the place.

As night falls, the port illuminates like a Christmas tree. Take a nighttime port boat excursion to get a new perspective on the city. Then, stop by one of the numerous pubs or cocktail bars in the vicinity. The Bard & Banker, set in a former bank, offers live music alongside its beers.

Victoria's Inner Harbour and Downtown are packed with adventures. It's a location where you may meet residents, learn about history, and plan your own urban trip. So tie up your walking shoes and dig in; Victoria is eager to show you a wonderful time.

Nanaimo's Old City Quarter

When you enter Nanaimo's Old City Quarter, you will feel as if you have journeyed back in time. This attractive old quarter is the pulsating heart of the city, full of character and tales waiting to be discovered.

Walking along the cobblestone streets, you'll come across wonderfully renovated historical buildings that now contain eccentric stores, charming cafes, and art galleries. Keep a lookout for the unmistakable yellow and red brick facades; they'll let you know you're in the correct area.

Hungry? You are in luck. The Old City Quarter is a cuisine lover's heaven. Gabriel's Gourmet Café serves a warm cup of locally roasted coffee and handmade pastries. If you're looking for something heartier, The Nest Bistro delivers farm-to-table fare that will make your taste buds sing.

For history enthusiasts, the Nanaimo Museum is a must-see. It's a veritable treasure mine of local tradition, from the area's First Nations origins to its coal mining boom. The staff is enthusiastic about their city and always ready to share a fascinating fact or two.

As the sun sets, the quarter takes on a whole new feel. String lights shine overhead, and the sound of live music emanates from taverns and clubs. Grab a pint of craft beer at the Crow & Gate Pub, a popular neighborhood hangout for excellent reason.

Shopping here is a far cry from the average mall experience. Look for antique discoveries at Lucid, where each piece has a story. Visit Lobelia's Lair for some magical vibes and unusual presents.

If you're fortunate enough to visit on a Friday in the summer, you're in for a treat. The Old City Quarter Farmers' Market brings life to the city streets. It's a busy event, with local vegetables, craft goods, and street entertainers adding to the celebratory mood.

Do not hurry through this neighborhood. Take your time, speak with the shops, and take in the laid-back island vibe. The Old City Quarter is more than simply a site to see; it is a place to experience. By the time you leave, you could be planning your next visit.

Remember, the greatest approach to finding the quarter's hidden jewels is to follow your curiosity. Turn down that quiet lane, look into that fascinating shop display, or follow the sound of the street performer. Every location in the Old City Quarter contains the possibility for an adventure.

Unique shops and local markets

The shopping environment on Vancouver Island is a treasure trove for individuals who enjoy browsing, bargaining, and bringing home unique treasures. From eccentric shops to bustling farmers' markets, you'll find lots of opportunities to test your shopping skills and score some genuinely unique treasures.

Let's start in Victoria, where Government Street is a popular shopping destination. This busy road is dotted with a diverse range of retailers, from high-end boutiques to eccentric gift shops. Visit Munro's Books, a local institution set in a beautiful Neoclassical edifice. Book enthusiasts may easily spend hours browsing the shelves and conversing with the experienced staff.

Lower Johnson Street, also known as LoJo by locals, is only a short walk away. This colorful street is home to a plethora of unique shops selling anything from vintage apparel to artisan jewelry. Keep a lookout for Smoking Lily, a unique small business that sells locally made and printed apparel and accessories.

For a genuine taste of island life, visit the Victoria Public Market on the Hudson. This indoor market is a foodie's dream, with the best of Vancouver Island's vegetables, baked delicacies, and artisanal products. Strike up a discussion with the merchants; they are always eager to tell the story behind their products.

Leave Victoria and head to the Cowichan Valley. This area is a beehive for artists and crafters, and you can find their creations at the Duncan Farmers Market. This vibrant market, which takes place every Saturday, is ideal for stocking up on local honey, handcrafted soaps, and one-of-a-kind ceramic pieces.

The Old City Quarter in Nanaimo is a must-see for shoppers. This attractive historic quarter is brimming with individual stores providing everything from gourmet delicacies to locally produced goods. Don't miss Hill's Native Art, where you can purchase real First Nations art and jewelry.

For an off-the-beaten-path shopping adventure, take a boat to Salt Spring Island. The Saturday Market in Ganges is a must-see, with over 140 sellers offering island-made and cultivated items. The market is sensory overload in the nicest sense, with everything from tie-dye t-shirts to organic lavender.

Back on the main island, Coombs Old Country Market is a unique visit that you won't want to miss. Yes, there are goats on the roof (you read that correctly), but the true attraction is the diverse mix of foreign cuisine, local crafts, and housewares within. It's ideal for finding one-of-a-kind presents or sweets to take home.

In Tofino, the vibe transforms into relaxed, surfer chic. Caravan Beach Shop offers locally made apparel and accessories that embody the essence of island living. For something truly unique, go to the House of Himwitsa Native Art Gallery, where you may buy magnificent pieces of First Nations art straight from local artisans.

No shopping guide to Vancouver Island is complete without mentioning the numerous farmers' markets that sprout up around the island. From the Comox Valley Farmers' Market to the Qualicum Beach Farmers Market, these weekly meetings are ideal for socializing with locals and stocking up on farm-fresh produce.

It's about the stories, people, and experiences you'll have while shopping on Vancouver Island, not just the goods you buy. So take your time, talk to the shops, and enjoy the relaxed island approach to retail therapy.

Shopping for souvenirs and local products
Vancouver Island has a flair for making shopping an adventure. Forget the typical tourist traps; this

business gives up unusual treasures that will fill your bag with local character.

First stop: Victoria's crowded streets. The capital exudes charm, and its stores do not disappoint. Wander down Government Street, where First Nations artwork draws your attention at every step. Carved masks, elaborate jewelry, and posters that tell stories about the island's rich past will make you want to free up some wall space at home.

However, don't blow your budget just yet. Head to Bastion Square, where the Sunday market is a wonderful trove of island-made goods. Chatty merchants sell anything from hand-poured candles to unique driftwood sculptures. Pro tip: get some locally roasted coffee beans; they'll brighten your mornings long after your tan has faded.

If you want something with more bite, head to Cowichan Bay. This little community is a foodie's heaven. Stock up on artisanal cheeses, small-batch preserves, and, if you're feeling daring, some very fiery homemade sauce. Your taste buds will appreciate you, even if your bags will not.

Nanaimo has something to offer craft beer enthusiasts. The city's developing brewery culture allows you to get some limited-edition brews to wow your pals back home. Just remember to pack them gently; nobody wants a bag that smells like a fraternity party.

Tofino, the surf town with soul, has its own kind of retail therapy. Skip the big brands and explore the little stores. You'll discover warm sweaters made from island wool, ideal for cool beach nights. Don't pass up the handcrafted soaps flavored with local seaweed; they're like carrying a bit of the Pacific home with you.

But here's a secret: some of the finest mementos don't come from stores at all. Keep an eye out for roadside vendors as you tour the island. That's where you'll find jars of golden honey direct from island hives, as well as lavender bundles that will keep your drawers smelling fresh for months.

And let us not forget about the markets. Farmers' markets are weekend staples everywhere from Duncan to Qualicum Beach. Load up on island-grown teas, small-batch spirits, and artworks depicting Vancouver Island's raw beauty. Talk to the manufacturers; they have tales that will make your purchases even more special.

Visit during one of the island's numerous festivities to create a genuinely unique souvenir. The Filberg

Festival in Colorado is a treasure trove of one-of-a-kind products, and the Cowichan Valley Wine Festival allows you to stock up on bottles that you won't find anywhere else.

Shop Vancouver Island style for more than just the goods—discover the stories along the way. So put down the guidebook for a while, follow your nose, and let the island surprise you. Who knows. That weird shell jewelry or unique driftwood lamp may become your new favorite conversation starter.

Just a word of caution: leave some space in your suitcase. When you start visiting Vancouver Island's boutiques, markets, and hidden jewels, you may find yourself wanting additional luggage for the trip home.

Chapter 7

Family-Friendly Activities and Attractions

Best Beaches for Families

Vancouver Island's beaches are a treasure trove for families wishing to create memorable experiences. Every clan will find the ideal location, from tranquil, secluded coves to broad stretches of beach.

Parksville Beach is popular with both residents and visitors. When the tide goes out, it leaves a large playground of warm, shallow ponds. Kids may swim about securely while their parents relax on the soft sand. The adjoining community park, which includes a big playground and splash pad, adds to the pleasure.

For a more adventurous experience, visit Long Beach in Pacific Rim National Park Reserve. This 16-kilometer stretch of shoreline will take your breath away with its sheer vastness. Beachcombing here is an adventure; you never know what riches the waves may bring in. Just keep a watch on the small ones, since the surf may be rough.

Tribune Bay on Hornby Island is known as the "Little Hawaii" of the north. Its crescent-shaped beach features crystal-clear waves and fluffy white sand. The bay's sheltered location ensures tranquil waters, ideal for family swimming. Pack a picnic and make a day of it; you won't want to leave.

If you're looking for a more private location, visit Miracle Beach Provincial Park. The beach here is pebbly, but it's ideal for making driftwood forts and discovering tidal pools. The neighboring woodland provides shaded pathways for times you need to get away from the sun.

Rathtrevor Beach in Parksville is another family favorite. At low tide, the water recedes about a kilometer, exposing a huge stretch of sand speckled with tidal pools. It's like nature's own science class; your children can see crabs, sea stars, and other aquatic creatures.

For families with older children looking for some excitement, head to Chesterman Beach in Florida. It's an excellent place for novice surfers, with calm waves and various surf schools nearby. Even if you don't want to ride the waves, it's fun to watch others try.

Qualicum Beach has a distinct atmosphere. This long, straight length of beach is ideal for leisurely hikes. The town is only a few feet away, so you can simply stop for ice cream or fish & chips when you're hungry.

Don't forget about the beaches near Victoria. Willows Beach in Oak Bay is a local favorite. Its tranquil seas and adequate amenities make it perfect for a family outing. There's even a tea cafe nearby for a civilized respite from the heat and sand.

Remember that Vancouver Island's weather may be unpredictable. Even on overcast days, these beaches provide plenty of entertainment. Bring layers, sunscreen, and a spirit of exploration. Whether you're building sandcastles, flying kites, or simply taking in the scenery, Vancouver Island's family-friendly beaches will serve as the background for some of your most memorable holiday moments.

Educational Experiences and Wildlife Centers

Vancouver Island has a wild side that will blow your socks off, and it's more than simply the landscape. This is a live, breathing school where you may get near and personal with nature's best.

Consider the Nanaimo Museum, for example. It's not your typical dusty old building full of antiquities. Nope, this location brings the island's history to life. You'll be strolling into a coal mine one minute and standing in a First Nations longhouse the next. It's hands-on history that will make you forget you're learning anything.

If you're looking for furry and feathered pals, visit the North Island Wildlife Recovery Centre in Errington. This is more than just a zoo; it's a full-fledged rehabilitation facility for injured and orphaned wildlife. You could observe a bald eagle having its wing repaired or a bear cub learning to forage. The employees here are enthusiastic about their profession and always eager to speak. Trust me, you'll leave with a renewed appreciation for animal protection.

Now, if you've ever wanted to be a marine biologist for a day, the Shaw Centre for the Salish Sea in Sidney is your chance. This site focuses on the Pacific Northwest's underwater ecosystem. You may interact with starfish, watch jellyfish dance, and even view a giant Pacific octopus up close. It's like plunging into the water without getting soaked.

But here's a true gem: the Bamfield Marine Sciences Centre. It's a little off the beaten route, but that's what makes it unique. This is a working research station where you may go on boat trips with genuine scientists, investigate tidal pools, and even contribute to ongoing studies. It's not only for scientific buffs; anyone with a keen mind will have a wonderful time here.

For a taste of island farm life, visit Morningstar Farm in Parksville. It is home to Little Qualicum Cheeseworks and MooBerry Winery. You may see cheese being produced, pet some friendly farm animals, and even milk a cow if you're feeling adventurous. It's an enjoyable and tasty way to learn about sustainable agricultural techniques.

We can't talk about educational experiences without including the Royal BC Museum in Victoria. This is a well-known museum. From the huge display to the model of Captain Vancouver's ship, you'll become lost in time. The First Peoples Gallery is extremely impressive, providing a completely new viewpoint on the island's indigenous past.

For a more challenging trip, the Goldstream Provincial Park Visitor Centre near Victoria is a must-see. If you time it correctly (typically in November), you'll be treated to one of nature's most amazing spectacles: millions of salmon battling their way upstream to spawn. The park rangers here are knowledgeable and can describe the entire lifecycle in fascinating detail.

Finally, don't miss the Quatse Salmon Stewardship Centre in Port Hardy. It's a little community with a big mission: safeguard the local salmon species. You may observe salmon at various stages of growth and even help release some fry into the wild. It's a hands-on method to grasp how important these fish are to the island's environment.

The educational experiences on Vancouver Island are not limited to gazing at items behind glass. They encourage getting your hands dirty, asking questions, and perhaps even helping out. Whether you're a nature lover, a history buff, or simply interested in the world around you, you'll find something here that will pique your curiosity and perhaps teach you something along the way.

Amusement parks and recreational facilities

When it comes to amusement parks and recreation areas, Vancouver Island has a lot of fun to offer. You wouldn't expect this nature lover's paradise to be beehive of thrills and spills, but you'd be surprised.

Consider WildPlay Element Parks in Nanaimo, for example. It's not your typical playground. Imagine yourself zooming through the treetops, your heart beating as you traverse airborne obstacle courses. The Monkido Aerial Adventure course is popular among both children and adults who regard themselves as modern-day Tarzans. If you truly want to test your boundaries, attempt the What's To

Fear Jump, a 150-foot freefall that will make you reconsider your life choices (in the best manner imaginable).

For a more relaxed day out, visit Parksville. The Riptide Lagoon Adventure Golf is a mini-golf course that puts the 'fun' in quirky. With its zany hurdles and whimsical themes, it's ideal for some family-friendly competition. Just don't get too wrapped up in the game; the view is really spectacular.

If you have young children, Paradise Fun Park in Parksville is a must-see. It has all of the usual amusements, like bumper boats, go-karts, and an arcade that will keep the kids (and, let's be honest, adults) delighted for hours. The mini-golf course here is also really unique, with waterfalls and other interesting features to liven up your putting game.

Horne Lake Caves Provincial Park is a unique place to visit. Okay, it's not really an amusement park, but listen to me. The guided cave explorations here are like nature's own adrenaline rush. Squeezing down tiny corridors, scrambling over boulders, and exploring subterranean waterfalls is an adventure you won't soon forget.

If you prefer more conventional outdoor activities, Vancouver Island has a wide range of options. The Juan de Fuca Provincial Park has some of the greatest hiking routes around. The Juan de Fuca Marine Trail is particularly noteworthy; it's difficult, but the coastline views make every step worthwhile.

Water enthusiasts have plenty of alternatives. Tofino is world-renowned for its surfing, with locations perfect for everyone from complete beginners to seasoned pros. If you've never attempted catching a wave before, there are many surf schools in town that will have you standing up (hopefully) in no time.

Kayaking is another popular pastime, particularly around the Gulf Islands. Grab a paddle and explore secluded coves; look for seals lazing on rocks; and if you're lucky, you could catch a glimpse of an orca pod.

Mountain bikers, listen up. The trails surrounding Cumberland are garnering recognition as some of the greatest in North America. With almost 80 kilometers of singletrack winding through lush forests, it's a two-wheeled heaven. Even if you aren't into rough downhill riding, there is plenty of simpler terrain to enjoy.

For a more casual day out, why not try disc golf? The course in Bowen Park in Nanaimo is free to play and provides an enjoyable challenge for all skill levels. It's a terrific way to enjoy the outdoors without breaking a sweat (until your competitive side takes over).

Vancouver Island may not have the big theme parks seen in other areas of North America, but what it lacks in rollercoasters, it more than compensates for in unique experiences and natural thrills. Whether you're speeding through the treetops, discovering underground caves, or simply enjoying a round of mini-golf with a view, you'll have a wonderful time. Enjoy yourself—that's what the holidays are about, right?

Family-friendly tours and activities

Vancouver Island is a family playground, full of activities that will make both children and adults happy. You'll have plenty of opportunity for adventure, learning, and bonding here.

Visit the Butterfly Gardens in Victoria. It's like walking into a tropical paradise with free-flying butterflies all around you. Children may observe these beautiful insects up close, and if they're lucky, a butterfly may even rest on their shoulders! The gardens also have flamingos, exotic birds, and poison dart frogs (safely behind glass, of course).

The Shaw Centre for the Salish Sea in Sidney offers a blend of education and entertainment. This hands-on aquarium allows youngsters to interact with starfish, sea urchins, and other tidal pool critters. What is the best part? The experienced staff is always ready to answer the countless "why" inquiries that children love to ask.

Do you like to spend the day learning about history while also playing outside? Explore Fort Rodd Hill and Fisgard Lighthouse National Historic Sites. Children may explore historic military defenses, pretend to be lighthouse keepers, and run across green meadows with the ocean as a backdrop. Bring a picnic and make a day of it!

If your family likes animals, don't miss the North Island Wildlife Recovery Centre in Errington. It's not your usual zoo; this facility rescues and rehabilitates wild creatures. You could spot bears, eagles, and owls up close. The staff's enthusiasm for animals is contagious, and your children will leave with a renewed awareness for environmental conservation.

Beacon Hill Children's Farm in Victoria offers a taste of farm life. It's popular with children, who can handle goats, feed chickens, and see the famed "running of the goats"—a daily ritual in which the goats enthusiastically hurry to their nocturnal enclosure.

Are there any thrill seekers in the family? Visit WildPlay Element Parks in Nanaimo or the Comox Valley. Ziplines, aerial games, and bungee leaps provide enough adrenaline-pumping activity to exhaust even the most active children (and adults!).

On wet days (hey, it's the Pacific Northwest after all), the British Columbia Forest Discovery Centre in Duncan is an excellent indoor-outdoor destination. Take a train trip into the forest, view historic logging equipment, and learn about the island's forestry history in an engaging way for children.

A whale-watching excursion departing from Victoria, Tofino, or Campbell River provides a one-of-a-kind island experience. The expression on your children's faces when they see their first orca or humpback whale? Priceless. Many tour companies provide family-friendly journeys with marine scientists on board to answer all your queries.

Beach days are essential on Vancouver Island. Parksville and Qualicum Beach are ideal for families, with warm, shallow seas and plenty of sandcastle-building options. During the summer, visit the Parksville Beach Festival, where professional sand sculptors create stunning works of art.

The Coombs Old Country Market offers a day of old-fashioned enjoyment. Yes, that's the home with goats on the roof! After watching the goats graze, visit the market's unique stores, eat some ice cream, and let the kids run about on the large playground.

Don't forget about the island's fantastic hiking paths. Many are family-friendly, such as the short stroll to Little Qualicum Falls or the simple loops in

Goldstream Provincial Park. These pathways provide huge rewards for little effort, with roaring waterfalls and towering trees that will make your children feel like they're in a magical forest.

Family activities on Vancouver Island are about more than just entertaining children; they are also about making memories together. Whether you're making sandcastles, watching whales, or exploring woods, you're bound to find something that will have the entire family talking about your island vacation for years.

Chapter 8

Practical Information for Visitors

Local Laws and Etiquette

Welcome to Vancouver Island, where the relaxed West Coast atmosphere meets Canadian friendliness. The residents are nice, but there are a few unwritten rules to follow if you want to fit in.

First and foremost, let's address the major issue: smoking. British Columbia has some of the most stringent anti-smoking legislation in Canada. You cannot light up in public buildings, workplaces, or within 6 meters of entrances, windows, or air intakes. This covers electronic cigarettes and vaping. If you smoke, you'll need to find authorized smoking sites or stay in private.

Now, when it comes to alcohol, the island is less strict than certain places in Canada. You may purchase alcohol at liquor stores, grocery stores, and even neighborhood stores. But don't get any bright ideas about cracking open a cold one in public; drinking on the streets or in parks is strictly prohibited unless special event permission is obtained.

Speaking of parks, Vancouver Island is an outdoor enthusiast's dream. Remember, with tremendous beauty comes enormous responsibility. Stick to established routes, pack out what you bring in, and, for goodness sake, don't feed the wildlife. Those charming raccoons may appear hungry, but feeding them is dangerous for their health and your cash if caught.

Driving on the island? Keep a lookout for wildlife on the roadways, particularly at dawn and twilight.

Oh, and leave your phone alone when driving; using portable gadgets behind the wheel is banned, and the penalties are steep.

When it comes to social conventions, Islanders are quite relaxed. However, there are several factors to bear in mind. Personal space is important, so avoid getting too near when conversing with natives. A pleasant nod or a "hey" is usually sufficient while passing strangers on the street.

Tipping is customary in restaurants, pubs, and for services like cabs or haircuts. The normal amount is 15-20% of the pre-tax cost. When you're welcomed to someone's house, it's customary to provide a little gift, such as wine or chocolates.

Environmental awareness is high here. Use reusable shopping bags instead of plastic bags, as many businesses charge for them. Recycling and composting are treated seriously, so follow the waste-sorting guidelines.

LGBTQ+ visitors will find Vancouver Island warm and accepting. Same-sex marriage is legal in Canada, and discrimination based on sexual orientation or gender identity is strictly outlawed.

If you have the opportunity to visit First Nations communities or attend cultural events, please obtain permission before taking pictures, particularly of ceremonial artifacts or performances. Listen more than you say, and be willing to learn about the island's many indigenous traditions.

Finally, a word about cannabis. Yes, it is legal in Canada, but it does not imply that it is free for all. You cannot smoke it anywhere you like; the same regulations apply to tobacco. And don't even think about attempting to get it across the border when you depart.

Remember, the secret to enjoying Vancouver Island is to unwind and go with the flow. Treat the island and its people with respect, and you'll fit right in with the laid-back island culture. Now get out there and explore; the island is waiting for you!

Health and Safety Tips

Hello, there, fellow travelers! Before you pack your bags and travel to Vancouver Island, let's talk about how to be healthy and safe. Trust me, a little planning goes a long way toward ensuring that your island vacation goes off without a hitch.

First things first: the weather. Climate-wise, Vancouver Island has a bit of a divided personality. The Eastern Side? Pretty mild. But what about the western coastline? That's where things can go crazy.

Pack for all seasons, even if you're traveling in the summer. A decent raincoat and durable boots are your greatest allies here. The weather may change on a dime, so always check the forecast before leaving for the day.

Now let us chat about the magnificent outdoors. Vancouver Island is a nature lover's delight, yet Mother Nature requires respect. If you're hitting the trails, let someone know where you're going and when you'll return. Better yet, team up. Solo trekking may seem romantic, but it is not worth the danger. Stick to established paths and bring a map; your phone's GPS may fail you when you need it the most.

Speaking of fauna, Vancouver Island has some spectacular residents. Bears and cougars make this location home; therefore, practice animal safety. Make noise when hiking to prevent startling any furry pals. If you approach a bear, be calm, talk quietly, and back away slowly. Never flee; you can't outrun them.

Water safety is also crucial here. The Pacific is beautiful, but those waves pack a punch. If you're not a good swimmer, stay at the supervised beaches. Tofino's surf seems appealing, but if you're a novice, schedule a lesson with a professional. The currents can be unpredictable, and the water is cold year-round. A wetsuit is a smart idea, even in the heat.

Canada has universal healthcare; however, it is not free for tourists. Purchase travel insurance before leaving your home. It's a tiny fee to pay for your piece of mind. Pack any prescription medications you require, along with a copy of the prescription itself.

Food and water? Don't worry. Tap water is safe to drink around the island. The native cuisine is amazing, particularly the fish. But if you're eating raw oysters (which you should), make sure they're from a trustworthy source. Food sickness is no pleasant, especially on vacation.

One final thing: ticks. These little troublemakers are capable of carrying Lyme disease. If you're trekking through thick grass or forested regions, wear long pants and check yourself later. If you come across a tick, don't worry. Simply remove it gently and keep an eye on the bite area.

Remember that the emergency number in Canada is 911. Save it on your phone just in case. Don't let all of this safety stuff worry you. Vancouver Island is quite safe, and the people there are polite and always eager to assist. A little common sense may go a long way toward ensuring that your island experience is memorable for the right reasons. Now get out there and have fun!

Communication and WiFi access

Staying connected on Vancouver Island is simple, so you won't have to worry about missing those Instagram-worthy moments or losing touch with loved ones back home. The island's well-developed infrastructure ensures that Wi-Fi hotspots and cell coverage are available in the majority of populous places.

Many cafés, restaurants, and public locations in Victoria and Nanaimo have free Wi-Fi. Simply check for posters offering free internet or contact the personnel; they are typically willing to provide the password. If you love to read, public libraries are your best friend. You may not only peruse local literature but also use the computers and Wi-Fi for free.

Hotels and hostels often provide free Wi-Fi to visitors, albeit the quality varies. If you intend to work remotely or stream movies, you should read reviews or ask the hotel directly about its internet speeds.

Be prepared for poor service if you venture into more distant locations, such as the mountainous west coast or the island's north. Tofino and Ucluelet have excellent Wi-Fi in town, but once you reach the trails or beaches, your signal may fade quicker than a whale's tail fluke.

If you want consistent access, rent a portable Wi-Fi gadget or buy a local SIM card. The island is served by all of the major Canadian carriers, including Rogers, Bell, and Telus. Most convenience stores and carrier shops in major towns provide prepaid SIM cards.

For a really off-grid experience in areas like Strathcona Provincial Park, embrace the digital detox. Your vacation on Vancouver Island was to reconnect with nature, not your email.

Public phones are becoming more rare; however, they may still be found in several town centers and transit hubs. They come in helpful in an emergency, so have some spare change available.

If you are traveling from another country, check with your carrier regarding international roaming arrangements before arriving. Some provide reasonable packages for Canada, while others may leave you with a bill as large as a grizzly bear.

Remember, while it's tempting to post every detail of your island vacation online, don't forget to look up. The authentic Vancouver Island, with its towering cedars, thundering surf, and interested animals, is far more engaging than any social media feed.

Currency, banking, and tipping

Staying connected on Vancouver Island is simple, so you won't have to worry about missing those Instagram-worthy moments or losing touch with loved ones back home. The island's well-developed infrastructure ensures that Wi-Fi hotspots and cell coverage are available in the majority of populous places.

Many cafés, restaurants, and public locations in Victoria and Nanaimo have free Wi-Fi. Simply check for posters offering free internet or contact the personnel; they are typically willing to provide the password. If you love to read, public libraries are your best friend. You may not only peruse local literature but also use the computers and Wi-Fi for free.

Hotels and hostels often provide free Wi-Fi to visitors, albeit the quality varies. If you intend to work remotely or stream movies, you should read reviews or ask the hotel directly about its internet speeds.

Be prepared for poor service if you venture into more distant locations, such as the mountainous west coast or the island's north. Tofino and Ucluelet have excellent Wi-Fi in town, but once you reach the trails or beaches, your signal may fade quicker than a whale's tail fluke.

If you want consistent access, rent a portable Wi-Fi gadget or buy a local SIM card. The island is served by all of the major Canadian carriers, including Rogers, Bell, and Telus. Most convenience stores and carrier shops in major towns provide prepaid SIM cards.

For a really off-grid experience in areas like Strathcona Provincial Park, embrace the digital detox. Your vacation on Vancouver Island was to reconnect with nature, not your email.

Public phones are becoming more rare; however, they may still be found in several town centers and transit hubs. They come in helpful in an emergency, so have some spare change available.

If you are traveling from another country, check with your carrier regarding international roaming arrangements before arriving. Some provide reasonable packages for Canada, while others may leave you with a bill as large as a grizzly bear.

Remember, while it's tempting to post every detail of your island vacation online, don't forget to look up. The authentic Vancouver Island, with its towering cedars, thundering surf, and interested animals, is far more engaging than any social media feed.

Chapter 9

Off the Beaten Path: Hidden Gems and Unique Experiences

Lesser-Known Hiking Trails and Viewpoints

The true magic happens along Vancouver Island's hidden pathways and secret lookouts. Forget the crowded tourist attractions; we're talking about off-the-beaten-path destinations that will make you feel like you've wandered into your own private slice of heaven.

Consider the Elk River Trail, for example. This hidden gem in Strathcona Provincial Park is somewhat of a local secret. It's a strenuous 11-kilometer hike that will leave your legs burning, but believe me, it's worth every step. You'll go through old-growth woods, past roaring waterfalls, and, if you're lucky, see some Roosevelt elk. What about the viewpoint at the end? It's breathtaking—a view of jagged peaks that will have you reaching for your camera.

The Juan de Fuca Marine Trail is a wonderful option if you want something gentler on your legs. It isn't precisely unknown, but most people just visit the popular portions. Proceed to the calmer Chin Beach to Sombrio Beach stretch. It's a 9-kilometer coastal trek that will have you leaping over driftwood, peeking into tidal pools, and perhaps spotting a whale or two if you time it correctly.

If you're looking for jaw-dropping vistas, the Mount Arrowsmith Lookout Trail is your ticket. It's a difficult climb, no doubt about it, but the payoff is immense. On a clear day, one can see all the way to the mainland. Just be prepared for some climbing at the summit; it is not for the faint of heart.

For a really hidden gem, try the Ladysmith Holland Creek Trail. It's practically on the outskirts of town, yet as you step along the trail, you'll feel like you've escaped society. The walk around an ancient dam, traveling through beautiful forests and along gurgling rivers. Keep a lookout for the heart-shaped tree, which has become something of a local icon.

If you're looking for a multi-day adventure, the Nootka Trail is difficult to top. It's distant, rough, and wonderfully breathtaking. You'll need to organize boat transportation to the trailhead, but once there, you'll have four to five days of breathtaking coastal wilderness. Think deserted beaches, thundering seas, and nights spent camping beneath a starry sky.

For something different, travel to Qualicum Beach and look for the Little Qualicum Falls Trail. It's a short walk, but don't be fooled: the waterfalls along the route are very breathtaking. In the summer, you could even discover a swimming hole to cool yourself in.

Finally, there's the Mount Tzouhalem Ecological Reserve Trail. It's a Cowichan Valley local favorite, with stunning views of Cowichan Bay. Spring is especially beautiful here, with wildflowers covering the grassy hills. Just remember to follow the defined pathways; this is a protected environment, after all.

Remember, there's a reason why certain paths are lesser-known. They're frequently more difficult and poorly maintained than the popular routes. Before leaving, always check the weather, have enough water and snacks, and notify someone of your intended destination. And please leave no trace; we want to maintain these places immaculate for the next traveler who comes upon them.

The secret paths on Vancouver Island are more than just hikes through the woods; they are doorways to adventure, windows into the island's untamed core. So lace up your hiking boots, grab your map, and prepare to uncover the island's best-kept secrets. Who knows. You could even discover your own bit of Vancouver Island magic along the way.
Secluded beaches and coves.

You're in for a treat if you're looking for that ideal stretch of beach away from the masses. The shoreline of Vancouver Island is dotted with hidden gems that will make you feel as if you've discovered your own little paradise.

Let's start with Mystic Beach. It's a bit of a climb to get there, approximately a 45-minute walk through gorgeous woodland, but believe me, it's worth every step. When you emerge from the walk, you're welcomed by a beautiful crescent of beach, flanked by steep cliffs. There's even a waterfall that flows right into the shore. It's the type of setting where you want to pinch yourself to ensure you're not dreaming.

If you want a true experience, head to San Josef Bay in Cape Scott Provincial Park. It's up in the northern tip of the island, and getting there is half the pleasure. The trip takes you through some extremely tough terrain, but once there, you'll be rewarded with three kilometers of pristine coastline. Massive sea stacks loom near offshore, providing an ideal setting for photography.

Sandcut Beach, near Jordan River, is a little more accessible but still off the usual path. A short route leads down to a pebble beach with a tiny waterfall carved into the rocks. It's an excellent picnic place, and if you're lucky, you could even see local surfers surfing the waves.

Speaking about surfing, China Beach is a secret treasure that is beloved among board riders but remains beneath the radar of most tourists. It's part of Juan de Fuca Provincial Park and features a combination of sand and pebbles, driftwood, and, on clear days, vistas all the way to Washington's Olympic Mountains.

If you're vacationing in Victoria and want a quieter option to Willows Beach, come to Gonzales. It is nestled away in a quiet neighborhood and frequently missed by visitors. The tranquil waters are ideal for swimming, and the west-facing position ensures spectacular sunsets.

Consider visiting Nootka Island if you truly want to get away from it all. Only accessible by boat or floatplane, the beaches are likely to be empty. Friendly Cove, the point of initial encounter between Europeans and the indigenous Nuu-chah-nulth people, is particularly noteworthy. The golden sand beach is surrounded by lush woodland, and you can see the ruins of an 18th-century Spanish fort nearby.

Back on the main island, Miracle Beach Provincial Park offers a wonderful stretch of sand ideal for beachcombing. At low tide, the beach appears to stretch indefinitely, revealing tidal pools rich with marine life. It's popular with families, but there's plenty of room to choose your own peaceful corner.

Last but not least, let's discuss Little Tribune Bay on Hornby Island. Okay, technically it's not on Vancouver Island, but it's only a short boat journey away and too amazing to pass up. The beach is clothing-optional (just in case that's not your thing) and has warm, shallow seas ideal for swimming. The pristine white sand and driftwood huts create an atmosphere reminiscent of the Caribbean in the Pacific Northwest.

Remember that these remote areas are appealing because they are secluded. Always pack out everything you brought in, respect nature, and leave no trace. That way, the next fortunate beachgoer may appreciate these hidden coastal gems as much as you did.

Agritourism and farmstays

The landscape of Vancouver Island offers a plethora of farm-fresh pleasures. Forget about ordinary hotels; here, you may wake up to the soft clucking of hens and the scent of freshly made bread flowing through your snug cottage.

Take the meandering rural roads to Cowichan Valley, known as "Canada's Provence." You'll be surrounded by rolling hills covered with vineyards, orchards, and family farms. Merridale Cidery & Distillery provides a one-of-a-kind experience in their yurts, which are placed directly in the orchard. Sip handmade cider as the sun sets beyond the horizon, painting the sky in colors that would make any artist grab for a paintbrush.

For a hands-on experience, visit Healing Farm on the Saanich Peninsula. This thriving organic farm allows you to get your hands filthy in the best manner imaginable. Help collect eggs, feed sheep, or learn about beekeeping. The farm's rustic cottages provide an ideal getaway after a day of agricultural activities.

Yellow Point Farms near Ladysmith is a popular destination for families with children. The children may bottle-feed young goats and snuggle with fluffy bunnies. The farm's guest house, complete with a fully equipped kitchen, allows you to prepare meals using vegetables harvested fresh from the garden.

Morningside Estate in Metchosin is an excellent choice for people looking for a touch of luxury during their farm visit. This luxurious house features seaside views, an on-site winery, and even a truffle orchard. You may participate in the truffle search with their trained dogs, a totally unique Vancouver Island experience.

Foodies, listen up! Ashleigh's Farm B&B in the Comox Valley offers farm-to-table breakfasts that will make you reconsider your daily routine. Their handmade jams and preserves are so delicious that you could find yourself sneaking a jar home in your bag.

But it's not only about overnight accommodations; Vancouver Island's agritourism sector also provides several day trip choices. The Saanich Organics Box Cycle Tour allows you to bike through fields while filling your bicycle basket with fresh vegetables along the route. It's similar to a treasure hunt, except with vegetables as the reward.

For a unique agricultural experience, visit Sacred Mountain Lavender on Salt Spring Island. Schedule your visit for July, when the purple blossoms are at their height. The relaxing smell alone is worth the boat voyage.

Don't miss the busy farmers' markets that crop up all over the island. The Duncan Farmers Market is a Saturday morning fixture where you can talk to local farmers and try anything from gourmet cheeses to wild-foraged mushrooms.

Agritourism on Vancouver Island is more than just a chance to eat local food—it's a chance to connect with the land and its guardians. Whether you're milking a goat, collecting berries, or simply enjoying a farm-fresh dinner, you're contributing to the island's rich agricultural tradition.

Pack your wellies and hunger. Vancouver Island's farmers are eager to show you a side of island life that extends beyond beaches and hiking trails. Who knows. You could even leave with a renewed appreciation for the humble carrot and a strong urge to establish your own vegetable garden at home.

Volunteer Opportunities and Environmental Initiatives

Want to get your hands dirty while making a meaningful difference on Vancouver Island? You're in luck: this pocket of paradise is overflowing with opportunities to give back to the environment and the local community.

Take the Surfrider Foundation, for example. These ocean fighters are constantly on the hunt for beach cleanup enthusiasts. Imagine yourself wandering along Tofino's magnificent beaches, waste bag in hand, speaking with like-minded people as you help keep the coast clean. It's more than just picking up garbage; you'll learn a lot about marine ecosystems and the effects of plastics on our seas.

If you have a green thumb, the Comox Valley Project Watershed Society may be ideal for you. They are all about rebuilding estuaries and salmon habitats. You may find yourself knee-deep in muck, planting native plants, and feeling fairly positive about restoring life to these critical ecosystems.

For animal lovers, the BC SPCA Wild ARC in Metchosin is constantly looking for an additional set of hands. You may be bottlefeeding orphaned fawns one day and then rehabilitating wounded birds the next. It's hands-on, dirty, but really satisfying labor.

If you'd like to combine your environmental activities with some island exploration, look into the Juan de Fuca Trail Stewardship Program. You'll be maintaining hiking routes, building bridges, and sleeping beneath the stars, all while taking in some of the most breathtaking landscapes on the island.

For individuals who prefer urban settings, Victoria's Compost Education Centre provides an opportunity to get messy with worm bins and compost heaps. You'll leave with earth under your nails and a plethora of information about sustainable living techniques.

If you're coming during the salmon season, don't pass up the opportunity to help at Goldstream Hatchery. You can be counting fish, maintaining trails, or teaching tourists about these unique Pacific Northwest species.

The Raincoast Education Society in Trinidad offers a range of volunteer opportunities. From performing shorebird surveys to assisting with kid nature programs, there is always something intriguing going on.

Consider volunteering with WWOOF Canada (World Wide Opportunities on Organic Farms). Vancouver Island is filled with organic farms where you may swap your work for lodging, food, and a true experience of island life.

If you're more tech-savvy, the Habitat Acquisition Trust might benefit from your expertise. They are continuously asking for volunteers to help with GIS mapping for vulnerable habitats and social media marketing.

Last but not least, keep a lookout for upcoming Great Canadian Shoreline Cleanup activities. They occur all across the island and are an excellent opportunity to meet people, get some exercise, and leave the beaches cleaner than you found them.

Remember, these chances are more than just giving back; they are your ticket to exploring Vancouver Island like a native. You'll make new friends, uncover hidden gems, and get greater respect for this beautiful area. So roll up your sleeves, get out there, and make your visit worthwhile!

Conclusion

As you end this guide, take a minute to think about the journey you're about to go on—or the one you've just completed. Vancouver Island is more than simply a vacation; it's a living, breathing tapestry of wild beaches, historic forests, and thriving villages.

You will feel it as soon as your feet touch the island's soil—that unexplainable draw that has captivated tourists for years. Perhaps it will be the foggy mornings in Tofino, when surfers ride the waves beneath a pale sun. Perhaps it will be the serene beauty of Cathedral Grove, where towering cedars have stood watch for a thousand years.

Victoria's lovely streets may steal your heart, with history whispering from every corner. It might also be the friendly grins of people in a tiny coastal village who are eager to offer their favorite secret beach.

Remember that the genuine enchantment of Vancouver Island is found not just in its postcard-perfect scenery but also in the moments in between—unexpected meetings, the taste of freshly caught fish, and stories shared over a locally made beer.

This book is your key to discovering the island's mysteries, but the true adventure comes when you stray off the main road. So go ahead and take that meandering route, converse with that kind individual, and agree to that unexpected whale viewing expedition.

Vancouver Island is eager to amaze, challenge, and inspire you. It's a location that penetrates your skin and into your spirit. And fair warning: after you've seen its natural beauty and wonderful warmth, you could find yourself planning your next trip before you've ever gone.

So pack your spirit of adventure and your curiosity, and get ready to fall in love with one of the world's most enchanting destinations. Vancouver Island is more than simply a location you visit; it becomes a part of you.

Safe travels, and may your journey be full of surprises at every turn. Until next time, fellow adventurers!

Made in United States
Troutdale, OR
03/21/2025